North & North West London
Edited by Michelle Afford

First published in Great Britain in 2008 by:
Young Writers
Remus House
Coltsfoot Drive
Peterborough
PE2 9JX
Telephone: 01733 890066
Website: www.youngwriters.co.uk

All Rights Reserved

© Copyright Contributors 2007

SB ISBN 978-1 84431 460 7

Foreword

Young Writers was established in 1991 and has been passionately devoted to the promotion of reading and writing in children and young adults ever since. The quest continues today. Young Writers remains as committed to the nurturing of poetic and literary talent as ever.

This year's Young Writers competition has proven as vibrant and dynamic as ever and we are delighted to present a showcase of the best poetry from across the UK and in some cases overseas. Each poem has been selected from a wealth of *Little Laureates* entries before ultimately being published in this, our sixteenth primary school poetry series.

Once again, we have been supremely impressed by the overall quality of the entries we have received. The imagination, energy and creativity which has gone into each young writer's entry made choosing the poems a challenging and often difficult but ultimately hugely rewarding task - the general high standard of the work submitted ensured this opportunity to bring their poetry to a larger appreciative audience.

We sincerely hope you are pleased with this final collection and that you will enjoy *Little Laureates North & North West London* for many years to come.

For My Nana

O Hart
2008

Contents

Tahirah Thomas (11) 1

Chestnuts Primary School
- Jenelle Sauntey (8) 1
- Ella Parker-Barnby (9) 2
- Chiyan Lam (8) 2
- William (9) 3
- Najma Clise (9) 3
- Celine Best (10) 4
- Cynyee Wong (8) 4
- Sara Foukroun (7) 5
- Baris Coskun (8) 5
- Danielle Ifeama (8) 5
- Rasheed Kamara (8) 6
- Alliyya Bibi (8) 6
- Haja (9) 7
- Dori (11) 8
- Addison (10) 9
- Bobbie Dawson (10) 10
- Glenn (10) 11
- Alaya Begum (10) 12
- Ella Caldwell (9) 13
- Charlotte Sarjeant (9) 14
- Omari Green (9) 15
- Daniel (9) 16

East Acton Primary School
- Tay Freeman-Fox (8) 17
- Rianne Wiles (8) 17
- Abdigani Yusuf (8) 18
- Klaudia Piesko (8) 18
- Jessica McDonagh (8) 19
- Moheshia Afful-Brown (9) 19
- Eilidh Short (8) 20
- Sadaq Nuur (8) 20
- Sara Stewart-Thaxter (8) 21
- Daniel Ozokolie (8) 21
- Ayman Sekkouti (8) 21

Ellen Wilkinson Primary School

Rochelle Kioi (10)	22
Ellie Lewis-Johnson (11)	22
Bradley Collins (11)	23
Isha Johnson (10)	23
Yvonne Uzoka (10)	24
Vladas Navickas (10)	24
Marcus Clarke (10)	25
Tashala Lawson (10)	25
Rakhib Hoque (10)	26
Shaki Balogun	26
Emma Crisford (10)	27
Magdalene Ampomah Asante	27
Elizabeth Battle (10)	28
Daniel Okojie (10)	28
Nabeela Zaman (10)	29
Najma Ali (10)	29
Zuzanna Wnekowska (10)	30
Jeeshan Faisal (10)	31
Kamal Esty	32
Lewis James (11)	32
Edinam Cece Edem Jordjie (10)	33
Zarah Ali (11)	33
Mohammed Kharim (10)	34
Danielle Jolley (10)	34
Grantas Pacesas	34
Yusuf Islam (10)	35

Essendine Primary School

Zainab Khalil	35
Tarek Elmasri (8)	35
Qamil Pajaziti (8)	36

Hanover Primary School

Martha Bradbury (10)	37

Hereward House School

Timon Greaves (8)	38
Gustaf Ahdritz (9)	39
James Robinson (7)	39

Oliver Lloyd-Williams (8)	40
Markos Manolopoulos (8)	40
Tom Smeeton (8)	41
Nick Lucas (7)	41
William Fryer (9)	42
Oliver Hitchcock (8)	42
Oscar Noble (9)	42
Patrick McCabe (8)	43
Matthew Thal (8)	43
Alexander Butcher (8)	43
George Lane (9)	44

Larmenier & Sacred Heart RC School

David Gabra (9)	44
Joe Stapleton (10)	45
Chaudien Mwalimu (9)	45
Dominic Waluszewski (9)	46
John O'Neill (9)	46
Oliver Hart (8)	47
Emma Mitchell (8)	47
Stefan Camber (8)	48
Lucie Nagy (8)	48
Fraser Gibbs (8)	49
Amira Campbell-Zeid (8)	49
Naomi Bharwani (10)	50
Benito Leus III (8)	50
Maria Howard (8)	51
Lauryn Pierro (10)	51
Donn Guray (8)	52
Thomas Fee (8)	52
Molly Gurney (8)	53
Michael O'Connell (8)	53
Brigid McMorrow (7)	54
Sofia Rodrigues (8)	54
Odegua Williams (10)	55
Amy Hagan (8)	55
Karol Rybarczyk (10)	56
Francis Edwards (8)	56
Eleanor Hare (7)	57
Sophie Castillo (9)	57
John Henry Howard (10)	58

Julian Alegre (7)	58
Kristina Novakovic (9)	59
Louise Walsh (7)	59
Oluwafemi Fadeyi (9)	60
Olivia O'Sullivan (8)	60
Louise De Thomasson (9)	61
Agatha Warren (8)	61
Benedict McGonigal (7)	62
Ellie Merron (8)	62
Rebecca Hare (9)	63
Flora Fergusson (9)	63
Leandros Philiotis (11)	64
Niall Walsh (11)	64
Natalie Kelly (10)	65
Julia Trudu (8)	65
Jerina Neli (7)	66
Theresa Boyo (8)	66
Grace Galbraith (10)	67
Amy Cavanagh (8)	67
Calypso Eaton (9)	68
Joseph Ejere (7)	68
Jamie Storer (7)	69
Daniel Alegre (7)	69
Maia Ferguson (8)	70
Grace McWeeney (7)	70
James Ireland (9)	71
Stella Smith (9)	71
Thomas Whear (10)	72
Isabella Curtis (9)	72
Natalie Barroso (9)	73
George Whear (7)	73
Isabel Cook (7)	74
Melanie Espinosa (8)	74
Lequain Matthew (8)	74
Matilda Cook (9)	75
Cameron Steel (10)	75
Francesca Vernazza (7)	75
Joseph McWeeney (9)	76
Joseph Ragheb (9)	76
Miguel Navarro-Alvarado (9)	76
Georgia Novell (8)	77

Norland Place School

Stephanie Christenson (7)	77
Imogen Ginty	77
Helena Peacock (7)	78
Raphaella Redfern	78
Emilia Kalff	78
Georgina Lloyd Yorke (7)	79
Stella Boden (7)	79
Georgia Colfer (7)	79
Maddie Dye	80
Lola Rawding (7)	80
Charlotte Soanes (7)	80
Orla Choo (7)	81
Charlotte Benigni (8)	81
Eugénie Bakker (7)	81
Helena Gray (7)	82

Princess Frederica CE VA Primary School

Jonelle Awotwi (8)	82
Tyrese Miller (8)	82
Rachel Sung Thomas (8)	83
Alice Such (8)	83
Rheshan Thompson (8)	83
Aysha Lohan (8)	84
Callum Burch (9)	84
Marko Pavlovic (8)	84
Jaymie Benka-Davies (8)	85
Teddy Otch-Imack (8)	85
Juan Carvajal Chalmin (8)	85
Ava Ansari (8)	86
Sabrina Wani	86
Magda Panek (8)	86
Daniel Oritsebemigho Olubanjo (9)	87
Ashleigh Mundle (8)	87
Ella Clarke (8)	87
Maisie Nutt (7)	88
Karina Ruseva (7)	88
Israel Awolaja (7)	88
Tabassum Ahmed (7)	89
Jack Batchelor (8)	89
Tom Smith (7)	89

Ashura Hirose (7)	90
Younes Benyamoune (7)	90
Finn Noble (7)	91
Asher Miller (8)	91
La-Tasha Jackson (7)	91
Lilly Smith (7)	92
Mahalia Mensah (8)	92
Aimee-Leigh Clare (7)	92
Rebecca Hollely (7)	93
Franz Elliah Gragasin (8)	93
Paris Brady Daley (7)	93
Freya Alexander (7)	94
Tuwuana Green (8)	94
Harry Wichman (7)	94
Annie Rose (7)	95
Georgie Charlton (7)	95
Estella Meachin-Taylor (8)	95
Jakob Leaf (7)	96
Jim Laney (7)	96
Ryan Hughes (7)	96
Maisie Macarthur (7)	97
Jerell Jeremiah (7)	97
Emma Coles (7)	97
Maya DeCosta (7)	98
Jade Read (8)	98
Milhaan Wani (7)	98
Bruno Bonacin (8)	99
Eden McNaught-Compass (8)	99
Louis James (9)	99
Deanna Webb (9)	100
Shania Alana Andall (8)	100
Luke Galvin (8)	101
Kieran Parchment (8)	101
Sadia Hameed (8)	101
Thaion Noel (8)	102
Vivienne, Caroline & Miranda (8)	102
Stanley Spark (8)	102
Marnie Hinds-Jones (8)	103
Noah Laignel (8)	103
Valexus Robinson (8)	103

St Christina's School, St John's Wood

Lily Goddard (9)	104
Francesca Histon (9)	104
Serena Eyi (9)	105
Molly Costello (9)	105
Sashini Ranasinghe (10)	106
Erika Shirai (9)	106
Yasmin Zouheiri (10)	107
Ines de Larrinaga (8)	107
Tamsin Taylor (9)	108
Ria Piccone (9)	108
Caroline Turner (10)	109
Camilla Tacconis (9)	109
Niku Hessabi (8)	110
Noor Jahanshahi (9)	110
Christina Marris (8)	111
Angelica Maxwell (8)	111
Ellie Marks (10)	112
Katharine Marris (10)	112
Sophia Jane Paravalos (8)	113
Francesca Morelli (8)	113
Laura Bouhélier (10)	114
Ava Meir (10)	115
Amanee Ekbal (10)	115
Martha Libri (10)	116
Nadia Muccio (9)	116
Kate Gardiner (10)	117
Victoria Harvey (10)	117
Minami Hashimoto (10)	118
Maria Rodriguez (8)	118
Callista McLaughlin (10)	119
Eleanor Shanahan (8)	119
Amy Pezzin (10)	120
Alice Johnson (8)	120
Willa Bailey (8)	121
Constance Marzell-Kyme (8)	121
Laura Pujos (10)	122
Lara Meir (8)	123
Ryoko Matsuda (8)	123

St George's (Hanover Square) School
Eloi Lopez Rodriguez (8)	124
Lethaniel Stacey-Coombe (7)	125
Callum Macleod (7)	126
Emmeline Crosby (7)	127
Shrawani Kulkarni (7)	127
Milos Petrovic (7)	127

SS Mary & Pancras CE Primary School, Camden
Christopher Docker (9)	128
Maisha Akter (8)	128
Rebecca Ahmed (9)	128
Libby Habib (8)	129
Hicham Medjebour (8)	129
Shannon Phelan (9)	130
Ellie Thompson (8)	131
Venetia Williams (8)	132
Samiya Rahman (8)	132
George Yoxall (8)	133
Salma Siddika (8)	133
Abby Webster (8)	133

Tetherdown Primary School
Tara Steeds (9)	134
Zak Tait (9)	134
Matthew Wickham (9)	135
Saskia Epstein-Tasgal (9)	135
Madeline Buttling-Smith (9)	136
Sebastian Jowett (9)	136
Robert Johnson (9)	137
Ben Long (9)	137
Ben Hodgson (9)	138
Julia Zlotnick (9)	138
Defne Navaro (9)	139
Murray Boyle (9)	139
Greta Shrimpton-Phoenix (9)	140
Cameron Wells (9)	140
Alice Martin (9)	140
Benjamin Levine (9)	141
Elinor Gibb (9)	141
Leo Style (9)	141

Joseph Humphreys (9)	142
James Hall (9)	142
Milo Nesbitt (9)	143
Jules Marks (9)	143

West Acton Primary School
Laura Latter (8)	144

The Poems

My Pets

I had a cat called Sella
She died, she died.
Mum said she was sleeping
She lied, she lied.
So I got a hamster at Christmas
She died, she died.
Mum said she was sleeping
She lied, she lied.
So I got a rabbit, Levi
He died, he died.
Mum said he was sleeping
She lied, she lied.
So I got a dog called Dragon
He died, he died.
Mum said he was sleeping
She lied, she lied.
Oh my, I had so many pets.
I hope they are all well in Heaven.

Tahirah Thomas (11)

The Snow

The snow is like crystals
Falling from the sky.
It is as soft as cotton wool
And as milky as a ghost.

It is as white as a skeleton
And as pearly as vanilla ice cream.
The snow pushes away the sun
To give us snow.

It is as bright and silky as cats' fur.
The snow is frost.
When it falls from the sky
And it passes by
It waves bye-bye.

Jenelle Sauntey (8)
Chestnuts Primary School

Wind

Howling wind and blowing hair,
Washing line gripping my underwear
It's blowing hard, the wind is bold
Makes my brolly impossible to hold,
As it blows inside out
It will break without a doubt.
Holding tight to my mother's hand
In case my feet lift off the land.
Ruffling my hair with invisible hands,
Like a giant hairdryer with many fans.
It blows leaves round and round
As they whirlwind towards the ground.
Howling down the chimney, rattling the doors
Like chattering teeth with a pause.
Wind breathing in my face
Then disappearing without a trace.

Ella Parker-Barnby (9)
Chestnuts Primary School

The Snow

The snow is like small balls,
Dropping from the sky,
It is as white as cotton wool
And it is a big pile of melted cream.

The snow wraps me up in its coldness,
It drops, melts and steams from the clouds
And it wanders through my window.
The snow is as cold as ivory.

Chiyan Lam (8)
Chestnuts Primary School

Please Mrs Gorph
(Based on 'Please Mrs Butler' by Allan Ahlberg)

'Please Mrs Gorph
This boy Charlie Choo
Keeps flicking me with a ruler, Miss
What shall I do?'

'Shut up, my darling
I don't care at all
Go and join the army
And come back for lunch in the dinner hall.'

'Please Mrs Gorph
This boy Charlie Choo
Keeps bullying me, Miss
What shall I do?'

'Punch him back, my love
Whack him with a cane
Do whatever you think is best
Cos I won't get the blame!'

William (9)
Chestnuts Primary School

The Snow

The snow is like small balls coming from the sky,
It is as yummy as vanilla ice cream,
And it is like white sweets rushing from the clouds.
The snow dances in front of me,
It steams, melts and dances in the street,
And it grabs me with its ice.
The snow is like white sheets flying through the air.

Najma Clise (9)
Chestnuts Primary School

Please Miss Potter
(Based on 'Please Mrs Butler' by Allan Ahlberg)

'Please Miss Potter
This boy is throwing rubbers at me.
Who is he?
Tell me, who shall he be?'

'His name is Mikey Moo.
Oh that silly moo.'

'Yes, Miss, it's that silly moo
That Mikey Moo.'

'Oh . . .ooh.'

'Miss, Miss.'

'Oh, what now?'

'It's Mr Pow Wow.'

'Oh, everybody hide
Before, oh no, he decides.'

Celine Best (10)
Chestnuts Primary School

The Snow

The snow is like candyfloss that falls from the sky.
It is as cold as the freezer
And it is soft like the kitten's fur.
The snow is water when the sun comes out.
Its temperature is coldness and it crunches
And it falls from the sky.
The snow is like a snowflake.

Cynyee Wong (8)
Chestnuts Primary School

My Bunny

I love my bunny's long ears,
Because they're the shape of wet tears.
I love my bunny's little nose,
Because it doesn't smell like someone's toes.
I love my bunny's tail,
Because it's not like a slimy snail.
I love my bunny's whiskers,
Because they're not sharp, dangerous killers.
I love my bunny's eyes,
Because they're like small flies.
I love my bunny,
Because it's so funny.

Sara Foukroun (7)
Chestnuts Primary School

The Sun

The sun is like a huge ball of lava floating high up.
It is as shiny as a brand new car
And a massive coin hanging in the sky.
The sun is a warm blanket
That goes and comes
And it shines like treasure.

Baris Coskun (8)
Chestnuts Primary School

The Snow

The snow is like bits of an ice cube,
It is as soft as cotton wool
And it is candyfloss falling from the sky.
The snow will touch the ribcage for warmth,
It is shiny, freezing, icy paper
And it will drop from up high.
The snow is as flattened as a ten pence coin.

Danielle Ifeama (8)
Chestnuts Primary School

The Snow

The snow is like water
And it is an ice cream.
The snow is white like paper.
It is cold, freezing and makes everyone cold
And it falls down on the Earth.
The snow is like the white powder on the top of a mountain.

Rasheed Kamara (8)
Chestnuts Primary School

The Snow

The snow is freezing vanilla ice cream.
It is as white as paint,
And it is a white sheet.
The snow is clear white.
It melts, touches and crunches,
And it will drop from the sky.
The snow is a snowflake.

Alliyya Bibi (8)
Chestnuts Primary School

Mrs Mahmoud
(Based on 'Please Mrs Butler' by Allan Ahlberg)

'Please Mrs Mahmoud,
This girl Grace Gobsmack
Keeps taking all my food,
Should I take hers back?'

'Flush her lunch down the toilet, lovely
Or tell a teacher on duty
I don't know, boil it pet
Leave me alone to sit on my booty.'

'Please Mrs Mahmoud,
This girl, Grace Gobsmack
Keeps being ever so rude,
Should I be rude back?'

'Go on holiday to Alaska, darling
Go across the Atlantic
If you have to doll
Just stop being so dramatic.'

'Please Mrs Mahmoud
This girl, Grace Gobsmack
Keeps being as rough as anyone could,
Should I be rough back?'

'Oh for heavens sake, love
Leave me be.
Fly away my dove
I want to drink my tea.'

Haja (9)
Chestnuts Primary School

Please Mr Bitler
(Based on 'Please Mrs Butler' by Allan Ahlberg)

'Please Mr Bitler
This boy Crazy Coo
Keeps hitting me, Mr
What shall I do?'

'Go and sit somewhere else, my son
Go and eat an ant
I don't care at all, dear child
Do whatever you want.'

'Please Mr Bitler
This boy Crazy Coo
Keeps flicking pencils, Mr
What shall I do?'

'Don't ask me, dear boy
I don't care at all
Do whatever you like, my puppet
Go and have a ball.'

'Please Mr Bitler
This boy, Crazy Coo
Keeps taking my money, Mr
What should I do?'

'Go jump out the window, child
Go on top of the roof
I don't care at all, son
Even if you lose a tooth.'

Dori (11)
Chestnuts Primary School

Please Miss Shaw
(Based on 'Please Mrs Butler' by Allan Ahlberg)

'Please Miss Shaw
This boy Shaun Shout
Keeps shocking me with electric pencils
Can you sort it out?'

'Go to the zoo, my dear
Go in a canoe
You'll find one in the teacher's car park
If you need me I'll be in the loo.'

'Please Miss Shaw
This boy Shaun Shout
Keeps hitting me with the ruler
Can you sort it out?'

'Snap it in half
Throw it away
I don't care, my dear
Just don't tell me today.'

'Please Miss Shaw
This boy Shaun Shout
Keeps poking me in the stomach
Can you sort it out?'

'Cut off his finger, dear
Send it to space
Become a singer
But don't leave a trace.'

Addison (10)
Chestnuts Primary School

Please Miss Georgiou
(Based on 'Please Mrs Butler' by Allan Ahlberg)

'Please Miss Georgiou,
This girl Lucy Loo,
Keeps on hitting me,
What shall I do?'

'Go the art room, my swan,
Take you books with you,
Bring a wallet, my love,
Don't boo hoo.'

'Please Miss Georgiou,
This girl Lucy Loo,
Keeps on cussing me,
What shall I do?'

'Go to the circus, my dear,
Always stay alone,
Never, ever come back, my buttercup,
Just take a bone.'

'Please Miss Georgiou,
This girl Lucy Loo,
Keeps on taking my pencil,
What shall I do?'

'Hide it in your pocket, my treasure,
Or eat it all the way down,
Never, ever bother me, my beauty,
Just never ever frown.'

Bobbie Dawson (10)
Chestnuts Primary School

Please Mrs Akarsu
(Based on 'Please Mrs Butler' by Allan Ahlberg)

'Please Mrs Akarsu,
This boy Colin Carew,
Keeps stabbing me with a pencil,
What shall I do?'

'Go and sit in the toilet, my honey,
Go and sit in the sink,
Go to the sea, my darling,
And let the sharks eat you.'

'Please Mrs Arkarsu,
This boy Colin Carew,
Keeps calling me Miss,
What shall I do?'

'Go and work in the hall, my dear,
Go and work beside the wall,
Go and sit in the toilet, my treasure,
I don't care at all.'

'Please Mrs Arkarsu,
The boy Colin Carew,
Keeps throwing the rubber,
What shall I do?'

'Keep it in your hand, my love,
Hide it in your car,
Sort it out yourself, my dear,
Throw it away to Mars.'

Glenn (10)
Chestnuts Primary School

Please Miss Potter
(Based on 'Please Mrs Butler' by Allan Ahlberg)

'Please Miss Potter
This girl Molly Moo
Keeps poking me on my arm, Miss
What shall I do?'

'Move somewhere else, dear
Wear metal under your vest
Bite her if you like for all I care
Do whatever you think is best.'

'Please Miss Potter
This girl Molly Moo
Keeps kicking my leg, Miss
What shall I do?'

'Tango if you can, my dear
Salsa if you like
Teach her if you want
Even go do it on your bike.'

'Please Miss Potter
This girl Molly Moo
Keeps beating me up, Miss
What shall I do?'

'Call her a big bully, love
Run to the biggest sea
Run home, my darling
But don't ask *me!*'

Alaya Begum (10)
Chestnuts Primary School

Please Miss Stickland
(Based on 'Please Mrs Butler' by Allan Ahlberg)

'Please Miss Stickland
This boy, Drake Deu
Keeps telling me to be quiet, Miss
What shall I do?'

'Run away to New Zealand, dear
Dress up as a chimpanzee
Go home and tell your dad, hun
Just don't bother me.'

'Please Miss Stickland
This boy Drake Deu
Keeps jogging me with my work, Miss
What shall I do?'

'Read a funny book, my treasure
Play Connect-4
Lock yourself in a cellar, darling
Don't ask me anymore.'

'Please Miss Stickland
This boy Drake Due
Keeps talking to me, Miss
What shall I do?'

'Go upon the roof, my love
Sail across the Atlantic
Take a trip to America, sweetheart
I think I'm going to be sick.'

Ella Caldwell (9)
Chestnuts Primary School

Please Mrs Mahmoud
(Based on 'Please Mrs Butler' by Allan Ahlberg)

'Please Mrs Mahmoud
This boy Sammy Sly
Keeps sticking his finger in my pie
Why does he have to be so sly?'

'Put it on his head, love
Go get a slice of bread
Whatever you do, flower
Just shoo.'

'Please Mrs Mahmoud
This boy Sammy Sly
Keeps flicking me with flies
It's not lies.'

'Catch them in your mouth, love
And run off south
Whatever you do, dear
Now there's a clue.'

'Please Mrs Mahmoud
This boy Sammy Sly
Is upsetting me with lies
No wonder they call him Sammy Sly.'

'Run to the staff room, my treasure
Run to your bedroom
Whack him on the head with a broom
Just leave me, with a *zoom!*'

Charlotte Sarjeant (9)
Chestnuts Primary School

Please Miss Potter
(Based on 'Please Mrs Butler' by Allan Ahlberg)

'Please Miss Potter
This girl Sevda Sais
Keeps poking me with a ruler, Miss
Oh my days!'

'Break it in half
Throw it away
Do whatever you want
But don't ask me today!'

'Please Miss Potter
This girl Sevda Sais
Keeps swearing at me, Miss
Oh my days!'

'Throw a tree at her, dummy
Throw her away
Sit in a corner
But don't bother me today!'

'Please Miss Potter
This girl Sevda Sais
Keeps drawing on my work, Miss
Oh my days!'

'Draw on her book, dummy
Throw yours away
But I told you before, pup
Don't bother me today!'

Omari Green (9)
Chestnuts Primary School

Please Miss Corphan
(Based on 'Please Mrs Butler' by Allan Ahlberg)

'Please Miss Corphan,
This girl Cocka Coodle-oo,
Keeps on throwing a rubber at me,
Whatever shall I do?'

'Shut up dear,
And run to the zoo,
Feed it to the cows, darling,
Until they go moo.'

'Please Miss Corphan
This boy Myron Meeshoo,
Keeps stealing my pencils,
Whatever shall I do?'

'Run away, dude.
Cos that boy's real uncool,
Disguise yourself as an old man, man
Using this ancient monocle.'

Please Miss Corphan,
This girl Dilshy Dranoo,
Is calling me rude names,
Whatever shall I do?'

'Lock yourself in a toilet,
Swim to France, mate.
Run from Spain to Germany
And duck behind my gate.'

'Please Miss Corphan,
This boy Tangrif Finlandu,
Is ruining my work,
Whatever shall I do?'

'Stop asking me!
As you can clearly see,
I need a wee and my tea!'

Daniel (9)
Chestnuts Primary School

Hurricane Poem

Petrified parents panicking,
Children stranded in the raging winds.
Drops of rain explode on rooftops.
Cars spinning in a whirlpool of mass destruction.
Demolished houses as far as the eye can see.
Thunder beats like echoing drums.

Screams of terror fill the air.
Boats being tossed around like paper boats.
Raging waters flood the roads.
Tangled wires bend like spaghetti.
Lightning pierces the darkness.
The hurricane rages on . . .

Tay Freeman-Fox (8)
East Acton Primary School

Hurricane

Terrified parents panicking.
Trees striking down houses.
Raging seas overflowing.
Lightning flashing like disco lights.
Screams of terror fill the air.
Demolished houses all over.
Tangled wires like spaghetti.
Raindrops pouring down.
Devastation spreads all over.
Howling winds shriek through the air.
Trees dancing the dance of death.
The hurricane is here to stay!

Rianne Wiles (8)
East Acton Primary School

Hurricane Poem

Petrified parents panicking.
The wind is as destructive as a volcano.
People screaming in the air.
Cars crashing!
Waves splashing!
Trees bending like elastic bands.
Howling winds blow houses down to the ground.
Lightning zigzags down to Earth.
Destructive tornadoes make big waves.
Thunder rumbles and roars.
Cars spinning!
Waves crashing!
Hurricane!

Abdigani Yusuf (8)
East Acton Primary School

Hurricane

Petrified parents panic
All around frantic fears fill the air.
Lightning flashes like disco balls
Exploding rain pours like sugar in a pot.
Children trapped under roofs blow away like feathers.
Thunder rumbling like drums.
Trees bend like elastic bands.
Tangled wires like cold spaghetti shudder in the cold.
The sea is now an exploding volcano.
Rivers start to overflow washing the city away.
Hurricane is *here!*

Klaudia Piesko (8)
East Acton Primary School

The Sea

Calm gentle waves crash on rocks
Shiny sunset relaxing after a long day
Golden sand shines through the crystal-blue sea
Feathery clouds blow away to make a lovely sunset.

Then suddenly without warning . . .

The sea lost control
Powerful waves crashed onto the shore
The huge sea crashes against ships and boats
Panicking people shout for help
Frantic cries fill the air
Oh sun, moody one, how can we live without your shiny face.

Jessica McDonagh (8)
East Acton Primary School

Crocodile And Me

Once I went to Africa,
To look and have some banana,
I stayed in a giant hotel,
But everything didn't quite go well.

A massive crocodile came running up to me,
As I was having my tea,
I smiled at the crocodile,
Then it smiled back a smile.

Me and the crocodile became friends,
Which will never ever end.

Moheshia Afful-Brown (9)
East Acton Primary School

Moody Sea

Gentle waves crash on the shore
Rainbow fishes dart through the crystal-blue water
Dolphins glide through the turquoise sea
Orange sunsets shimmer across the sky
Feathery clouds float across the blue sky
Then . . .
Angry waves consume everything in their path
Boats are tossed helplessly onto rocks
Frantic cries for help shatter the silence
The raging sea has lost control
Oh stormy sea, how can we live with your moody ways?

Eilidh Short (8)
East Acton Primary School

The Sea

Gentle waves crash onto the shore
Rainbowfish dart across the sapphire sea
Dolphins glide through the neon-blue sea
The orange sunset shimmers in the sea
Then suddenly, without warning . . .
Giant angry waves crash onto the shore
Waves consume everything in their path
Roaring waves crash on pitch-black rocks
Great boats are tossed helplessly around
Oh stormy sea, why are you so moody?

Sadaq Nuur (8)
East Acton Primary School

Hurricane

Powerful, zigzag lightning
Destructive as a volcano
Petrified parents panicking
Chaos everywhere
Vehicles crashing and splashing
Heavy rain pouring
Trees waving their hands
Splashing of sea waves
Strong winds
People shocked, screaming and hiding
The hurricane is here to stay.

Sara Stewart-Thaxter (8)
East Acton Primary School

Hurricane

Get some candles and fresh water
Shut your windows, lock your doors
Make a fire, get all cosy
Make hot chocolate
Yummy, yummy.

Daniel Ozokolie (8)
East Acton Primary School

Hurricane

Petrified parents panicking
Lightning zigzags through the dark sky
Howling winds crash through the cars
People running in terror and screaming
Thunder beating like drums
Mighty trees bend like elastic bands
Huge houses crash to the floor
The hurricane is here to stay.

Ayman Sekkouti (8)
East Acton Primary School

The Changes To The Weather

In spring the flowers start prancing like horses
It makes a soft singing noise like birds.
In spring everything is glamorous.
The blossom is colourful as a giant.

In summer the sun swims like children.
In the summer the sun starts skateboarding.
It makes a laughing noise.
The sun smiles at everyone.

In autumn the leaves jump off trees.
In autumn the leaves crunch like apples.
It breathes as loud as a bear.
The leaves walk like models.

In winter the snowman starts dancing.
In winter the snow freezes like a freezer.
The snow is like a crystal-white blanket.
Winter is like a booming giant.

Rochelle Kioi (10)
Ellen Wilkinson Primary School

Air

The air was dancing everywhere like a ballerina,
The air was swirling happy like a bird on a spring morning

It turned crazy like a lion,
And it twisted and hit the walls like a boxer,
The air was gushing sadly, like a grumpy old man,
As it sadly drifted off like a baby.

It ran out of the door and spun all over the place,
It faded in the darkness.
It flew over the mountains.

Ellie Lewis-Johnson (11)
Ellen Wilkinson Primary School

Black Hole

The black hole skipped all day long like a child on a pogostick.
The black hole extracted his voice as a snake hissed for a rat.
He gazed at the Earth like a hungry tiger.
He rushed at the speed of light.
All day he pounced at the moon like a grasshopper in a field
                                                        out in the open.
He jumped from planet to planet like a bouncy ball.
He was glamorous every day like a model walking down the catwalk.
He wanted as much food as a hungry sumo.
The black hole smiled with a cheesy grin.
Other planets were as amazed as teachers were.
The black hole was as demonic as a wild pack of wolves.

Bradley Collins (11)
Ellen Wilkinson Primary School

Sand

The sand was screaming and shouting.
It was terrified and scared and spinning in the air.
The sand was annoyed, it got a door and smashed it on the floor.

The sand was glamorous like a singer.
The luxurious sand was leaping like a frog.
It was fighting like thunder.
Then it was turning into snow
And it was devastated when it saw furious cars.
It was hot like a boiled egg.
The sand was fast like a cheetah.

Isha Johnson (10)
Ellen Wilkinson Primary School

The Compressing Whirlwind

The whirlwind rushed through my clothing like an X-ray going
through me.
The whirlwind was grinding on my skin like a hungry tiger.
A burning desire, it was possessed, forcing out its fierce smile.
The whirlwind was compressing the dunes of sand.

The whirlwind startled people all week.
The whirlwind looked like it was going to eat me.
The whirlwind gazed upon me.
The whirlwind was as fierce as a metal kettle pumping blood.

The whirlwind chased me like a cheetah.
The whirlwind crashed into a gleaming wall.
The whirlwind chased after my food like a crazy bird.

Yvonne Uzoka (10)
Ellen Wilkinson Primary School

The Grass

The grass was jogging like a hungry cheetah.
They started whispering
And smiling at me like a little girl.

The strong wind started blowing,
The grass was swinging.
They wanted to fly away
Like an owl but they couldn't.

The storm started,
It rushed like a jaguar chasing an antelope.

After the storm, the grass was as happy as a tiger
With his prey.

Vladas Navickas (10)
Ellen Wilkinson Primary School

Horrible Mr Twister

Mr Twister came to London
He was dancing around like a dancer.
He was eating all my food like a sumo
He froze London like it was the Ice Age.

Mr Twister went to the bank
He stole all the money like a robber.
Mr Twister was as sly as a fox
He became more famous than Kanye West.

He ate my roof like a hungry T-rex
He pounced to the military base.
He gobbled everyone there like a beast.
Mrs Twister was dashing to London.
Mr Twister hopped away and was never seen again.

Marcus Clarke (10)
Ellen Wilkinson Primary School

Storm

The suspicious storm smiles at me.
The superstitious wind grinned at me.
The horrid lightning shocked me
And the rain came down and soaked me.

The frightening thunder howled at me.
The heavy rain drowned me.
The wind from above froze me
And the storm came down and blew me.

The horrible storm cooled me down.
The sun came smiling upside down.
My mum picked me up and brought me home.
I sleep and sleep and sleep till dawn.

Tashala Lawson (10)
Ellen Wilkinson Primary School

Killer Rock

The killer rock is as colossal as a beast.
It rolls around and makes a spinning earthquake.
When the beast is angry it moans and groans all day.
It has a voice made with thunder and fire.

It somersaults off the cliffs.
Goes to people's food and sniffs.
The rock is a murdering beast.
It cries when it is hungry like an angry, hungry giant.

Its wrinkles grow larger and larger.
The rock threatens with its stormy eyes.
It runs as fast as a tornado.
It scratches with its claws.

The rock crashes through buildings and walls.
It crushes down windows and people in malls.
It rolls down fountains like Niagara Falls.
It gets strong when it drinks water, and . . .
The rock gets taller and taller!

Rakhib Hoque (10)
Ellen Wilkinson Primary School

Me

I know I have glamour and fame.
But some people gossip and say I am lame.
When midnight strikes I am on a mission.
I can smell two people that are not in a good condition.
I can see a girl that's so hideous.
I think I know her name, it might be Lillyous.
You may think this poem is not about me
But read it, in this poem I will set you free.
I will keep you from your pain and laughter.
You will live happily ever after.

Shaki Balogun
Ellen Wilkinson Primary School

The Glamorous Prancing Seashells

Seashells are prancing like a beautiful ballerina.
Seashells, seashells on the seashore eating like a grumpy pig.
Along jumped seashells wanting a cuddle.
The seashells are falling like a loving couple.

Along jumped seashells wanting a cuddle.
Seashells chatting about how amazing they are.
The seashells as smiley as the sun.
Seashells, seashells tap-dancing.

Seashells do the 'Cha Cha Slide'.
The seashells are more than happy to sing a beautiful song.
Seashells thank you for the kiss.
Seashells I love your dancing.
Seashells, come on let's travel around the world.

Emma Crisford (10)
Ellen Wilkinson Primary School

Beach Stones

The beach stones were swimming and rushing like an amazing starfish in the water.
The whole ocean was shining.
The luxurious sand was flowing into the water like a terrifying tiger.
And the big stone was magnificent like the ocean.
The jellyfish were flowing into the ocean like wonderful flowers.
The whole ocean was whispering like flying birds.

Magdalene Ampomah Asante
Ellen Wilkinson Primary School

Love

Love tastes like my dad's cooking
Love tastes like a chocolate cake
Love tastes like a big lasagne
Love tastes like cookies I love to make.

Love looks like a puppy sleeping in his bed
Love looks like bamboo growing from the ground
Love looks like my favourite shoes
Love looks like people walking in the town.

Love feels like a big hug
Love feels like sleeping in bed
Love feels like facing my fears
Love feels like my favourite ted.

Love sounds like my favourite song
Love sounds like people singing in the streets
Love sounds like people singing in a choir
Love sounds like people tapping their feet.

Love smells like a dozen roses
Love smells like a Christmas tree
Love smells like the waves of the sea
Love smells like fruit which, tastes good to me.

Elizabeth Battle (10)
Ellen Wilkinson Primary School

Football

Football is great with the wind in my hair,
The cheer from the crowd so loud I can't bear,
When I score a goal I feel ecstatic,
Football's physical but you need some tactics.

So never give and never be down,
People of tomorrow, this is your town,
Always remember that and you'll be fine,
And the world will be yours and mine.

Daniel Okojie (10)
Ellen Wilkinson Primary School

Thank You

Thank you for all I have to eat,
Thank you for every big treat.
Thank you for making me glad,
Thank you for my mum and dad.
Thank you for a place to learn,
Thank you for the money that I earn.
Thank you for a place to live,
Thank you for everything you give.
Thank you.
Thank you for teachers that care,
Thank you for the clothes that I wear.
Thank you for birds that sing,
Thank you for everything.
Thank you for adventurous places,
Thank you for meeting new faces.
Thank you for the air that I breathe,
Thank you for my munching teeth.
Thank you for gravity,
Thank you from me.
Thank you.

Nabeela Zaman (10)
Ellen Wilkinson Primary School

The Snow Days

The snow is clever as a cat.
It comes in December not November.
The snow is like a snowman.

Snow days are sad days.
The snow is as fast as a cheetah.
The snow is embarrassed like a person.

It is freezing like it is in Antarctica.
The snow is like fear of a lion.
The snow is shiny like diamonds.

Najma Ali (10)
Ellen Wilkinson Primary School

Feelings

Feelings look different,
Sometimes they look mad
But for real they are sad.
They can make you a
Different person for your whole life . . .

They don't taste the same.
They may upset you or even make you cry . . .
They could sound like a monkey's laugh,
But maybe like an elephant's cry.
When you see a happy person
You want to smile.

Feelings smell different,
Some good ones smell like colourful flowers,
But bad ones smell like
An old man's socks!

When you touch the good ones
They feel nice and soft.
Whenever you touch the bad ones,
They bite like a shark's teeth.

All feelings are different.
You don't know
How you will feel tomorrow . . .

Zuzanna Wnekowska (10)
Ellen Wilkinson Primary School

Magic

My name is Jeeshan
I am an amazing magician.
I get my fantastic wand
And I wish to swim in a tremendous pond.

I wish for a wonderful label
Instead I got a marvellous table.
I make a coin disappear
Then I make it reappear.

I make a girl go to sleep
Then I tell her to wake up with a loud beep.

I make a trick
With a brick.
It doesn't fall
But smashes the wall.

I built a magical house
I ran upstairs and wore a brilliant blouse.
Then I ran downstairs
And saw some magical bears.

I made a magical book
But no one ever looked.
I saw a magical box
And out came a terrific fox.

Jeeshan Faisal (10)
Ellen Wilkinson Primary School

Anger

Anger feels like squeezing my heart
I'm so angry far apart
Inside my skin.

Anger smells like melted chocolate
I am like an electronic associate
Inside my skin.

Anger tastes like plain rice
It's not good, it's not very nice
Inside my skin.

Anger sounds like babies crying
I want to help, I start trying
Inside my skin.

Anger looks like armies fighting
It's in my head, it looks like lightning
Inside my skin.

Kamal Esty
Ellen Wilkinson Primary School

Life

The hot sun's shining
When
Bright people are smiling.

When you're trying
You
Need a little bit of lying.

When there's a rainy day
It
Sometimes pays.

Because life's beautiful.

Lewis James (11)
Ellen Wilkinson Primary School

I'm . . .

I'm like a star shining in the sky
I am glistening like the clear blue sea
I am like a star falling, shining by
I am like a flower singing a melody.

I'm a child who likes different things
I am a girl who plays and sings
I am shiny as the yellow sun
I am a girl who likes to have fun.

I am elegant as I fly away
Today is the day, it is the day
For me to finally see
Today is the right day for me to be me.

Edinam Cece Edem Jordjie (10)
Ellen Wilkinson Primary School

What's That Smell?

The teacher passed out and fell right off her chair.
My classmates are crying and gasping for air.
The hamster is howling and hiding his head.
The plants by the window are practically dead.

There's gas in the class, it's completely my fault,
And smells like a chemical weapons assault.
Is it the smelly socks that are giving us shocks,
Or is it the fish on the docks?
I now know what it is, take it from me,
Don't take your shoes off after PE.

Zarah Ali (11)
Ellen Wilkinson Primary School

Embarrassed

When the feeling passes your blood
The shame makes you run away.
It looks like a volcano erupting on you
A volcano of laughter.

It smells like baby food for an 11-year-old
Which isn't meant to be.
It sounds like laughter
Everywhere you go, they're laughing at you.
Laughter, laughter!

It tastes like baby food
Getting fed by your mum
In front of everyone.
Baby food for an 11-year-old.

Mohammed Kharim (10)
Ellen Wilkinson Primary School

Glamorous

Glamorous tastes like chocolate melting in a pan.
Glamorous smells like air.
Glamorous sounds like the sea.
Glamorous feels like my cuddly toy.
Glamorous looks like my bed.
Glamorous is the best.

Danielle Jolley (10)
Ellen Wilkinson Primary School

Fun

Fun feels like swings
Fun tastes like sweets
Fun looks like slides
Fun sounds like rides
And fun smells like ice cream in the park.

Grantas Pacesas
Ellen Wilkinson Primary School

The Storm

My expression is like thunder.
My stare is like lightning.
My feelings are like the rain.
My whisper is like a chilly wind.
The storm is starting.
The storm is hard.
The storm is like a fire.

Yusuf Islam (10)
Ellen Wilkinson Primary School

Fireworks

Fireworks are shiny
And some are very tiny.
I have seen fireworks that are pink
That were in the sink.

Fireworks go all the way to the top
And end with a big great *pop!*
I saw a firework that wanted to
But there was not enough room.

Zainab Khalil
Essendine Primary School

Fireworks, Fireworks

I saw a firework that was pink
What other colours can you think?
Fireworks, fireworks in the sky.
Fireworks, fireworks oh so high
Fireworks make so much sound
They are very, very loud.
Blue, yellow, red and gold.
Sparklers are the best to hold.

Tarek Elmasri (8)
Essendine Primary School

Simple Rhyming A, B, C

A is for apple, ready to eat
B is for boots, to put on your feet
C is for cat, sitting alone
D is for dog, eating a bone
E is for eggs, all the same size
F is for frog, with big staring eyes
G is for gate, painted bright red
H is for hat, to put on your head
I is for insect, with six little feet
J is for jelly, wobbly and sweet
K is for keys, kept on a ring
L is for lamb, born in the spring
M is for mouse, eating some cheese
N is for nest, that swings in the breeze
O is for octopus, who lives in the sea
P is for pig, who cries wee, wee, wee
Q is for queen, wearing a crown
R is for rabbit, all white and brown
S is for sun that shines in the sky
T is for towel that soon gets you dry
U is for umbrella, to hold over your head
V is for van, bringing in the bread
W is for web, where a spider hides
X is for X-ray, which shows your insides
Y is for yellow, the colour of this wall
Z is for zip, our last letter that's all.

Qamil Pajaziti (8)
Essendine Primary School

Autumn

The soft light falls;
The dark nights silently call.
Towering trees cast,
Deathly shadows of the past . . .

Autumn is coming,
Coming, coming.
Autumn is coming day by day
Night by night
Until it's all gone!

The gentle wind blows;
Shatters the leaves on the trees, high and low.
It forms a golden shower that glides down
Of red, green, yellow and brown!

Autumn is coming,
Coming, coming.
Autumn is coming day by day
Night by night
Until it's all gone!

Fountains and lakes through rocks twist and twine
Sparkling like little stars shine.
The stars at night are like a sprinkle
Of salt on a Prussian blue cloth, twinkle, twinkle.

And in the morning the air
Is of smoky breath causing mist
And you go home and whisk
The hot chocolate!

Autumn is coming,
Coming, coming.
Autumn is coming day by day
Night by night
Until it's all gone.

The sunlight is mellow
It crystallises the dewdrops making them yellow.

Autumn is coming,
Coming, coming.
Autumn is coming day by day
Night by night
Until it's all gone
And white blankets of snow
Take over and sparkle half the world.

Martha Bradbury (10)
Hanover Primary School

Rugby Gladiator

Muscular men in position, crowds roaring
Like a pack of hungry lions from high above
Hearts thumping like bass drums
Sportsmen are leathery rhinos on the battlefield

Fired up fighters feel the heat
From the stadium lights.
Robust robots programmed to win
On the manicured greenery

The whistle, the fight begins
The English army takes force
And blasts the ball into electrified space

The pristine white shirts have gone now
Splattered with sweat and mud
Like galloping horses towards the precious ball

Swaying crowds singing, swing low
The final whistle goes.
Bruised French gladiators collapse on the muddy battlefield
As English warriors rise victorious (14-9).

Timon Greaves (8)
Hereward House School

The Palace

The palace is an ancient thing
Over a thousand years old!
With golden doors and marble floors
It's right to call it grand.
With many reliefs and fifteen chefs
With jewellery of every brand.
'The place is packed with expensive stuff,'
Says the queen, 'This is no bluff!'
'The Banquet Hall is way too small,'
Says the king and yet it's huge.
But if you ever come visit the place
You will be amazed by its grace.

Gustaf Ahdritz (9)
Hereward House School

What Is . . . ?

What is green?
Leaves are green, haven't you seen.
What is blue?
Waves are blue, crashing right through.
What is yellow?
The sun is yellow, in the morning it says hello.
What is red?
Hair is red, on top of your head.
What is white?
Snowflakes are white, glistening and bright.
What is gold?
Rings are gold, Saturn's rings you cannot hold.

James Robinson (7)
Hereward House School

England

Exciting England where I live,
Lots of amazing tourist attractions,
The Gherkin, Tower Bridge and Big Ben.
The Roman Baths are useful to learn about the olden days.
England is fabulous at sport, last night was spectacular.
England is full of parks to play sports in.
The buildings in the city are tall and proud,
Whilst the fields in the countryside are smooth and great to play on.
The people in England are kind, warm and inviting.
The food in England is fantastic,
Fish and chips our speciality.
I have visited countries all over the world,
USA, Colorado, Italy, France, Hong Kong, India and Jamaica
But England is my favourite place by far.

Oliver Lloyd-Williams (8)
Hereward House School

A Cold Winter's Morning

Frost falls from the Christmas trees.
The local ponds are frozen.
It's time for ice-skating and having lots of snowball fights.
The red berries.
Santa's presents and his reindeers.
His sleigh twinkles in the dark skies of winter
And in the morning we decorate the tree
And just before we go to bed we put out carrots and milk
And that is a cold winter's morning.

Markos Manolopoulos (8)
Hereward House School

The Tortoise

I am very slow because my house is on my back,
My skin is cracked and gums are hard,
I amble with my friend the snail,
I give the slugs fast rides on my back.
In summer I become a lot faster and my legs start to spin,
I circle the barbecue soaking in the sun,
While the giants cook their food.
All I want is crunchy lettuce.
The leaves fall and the wind roars.
When the foxes prowl I tuck up in my shell.
Now winter's here I search for a place to sleep,
Down into the flower bed I dig . . .
I am proud to be a tortoise,
And I am a hundred years old!

Tom Smeeton (8)
Hereward House School

The Flowers On The Table

The flowers on the table
Some are red, some are yellow, some are pink.
Flowers smell lovely like my mum and dad, they look beautiful
I hope they grow again.

Nick Lucas (7)
Hereward House School

The Mary Rose

We went to see the Mary Rose,
King Henry's fighting ship.
The ship was wrecked and split in half,
A huge wave made it tip!

'Oh no,' called Henry, how he wept
To see his treasure sink.
All the sailors were swept aside
Into the massive drink.

The ship was raised and sprayed with wax
And brought to Portsmouth Bay.
King Henry's ship is there to see
For hundreds every day.

William Fryer (9)
Hereward House School

Tennis

T actics are essential to winning
E verybody can play
N ot everybody enjoys it
N ets are the things you hit the ball over
I t involves a lot of running
S erving is the way to start each point.

Oliver Hitchcock (8)
Hereward House School

The Tiger

T he tiger is a brilliant hunter.
I ts claws razor-sharp.
G reat sense of smell the tiger has.
E verybody fears the tiger.
R unning along at amazing speeds.

Oscar Noble (9)
Hereward House School

Volcanoes

V olcano eruptions!
O n land and in the sea.
L ava pouring everywhere!
C ould you survive?
A shes block out the sunlight!
N o one can see!
O nlookers killed by flying rocks!
E verywhere,
S ome people survive . . .

Patrick McCabe (8)
Hereward House School

Dragons

D angerous beasts, when they
R oar the ground trembles
A cross the mountainside
G igantic, some really are
O range and red flames burst from their mouths
N otorious for their hunting abilities
S laying those who dare attack.

Matthew Thal (8)
Hereward House School

Maths

M ental maths is my favourite
A ddition is my second best
T ables are very nice
H undreds, tens and units are easy to use
S even is my favourite number.

Alexander Butcher (8)
Hereward House School

The Weirdest Animal On Earth

In Eastern Australia with the eternal summer,
Lives a weird animal.
It is not a beaver nor is it a duck,
It lives in a hole like a vole,
It swims like a beaver, where it borrowed its tail,
With a mouth like a duck,
Lays eggs like a bird,
Has hair like a mammal,
Have you guessed what it is yet?
It is a duck billed platypus!

George Lane (9)
Hereward House School

All The Creatures Of The Earth

All the creatures of the Earth
Are a wonder to the eye
From a lion's roar
To a mouse's squeak.
From a monkey in the trees
To a beetle on the ground.
All the creatures of the sea
Are a wonder to the eye
From the squeaking of the dolphin
To the humming of a whale.
From the salmon in the river
And the shark in the sea
All the creatures of the world
Are a wonder to the eye.

David Gabra (9)
Larmenier & Sacred Heart RC School

TV

TV is the best thing ever
It keeps you amused whatever the weather
We have a great big TV screen
It's the biggest thing I've ever seen.
Something you watch can be funny or sad
Other times it shows good things or bad
Documentaries, films and news
Are some of the channels we can choose.
My mum likes to watch the soaps
My sister likes the children's shows
Dad watching anything that's old
His favourite channel is UK Gold.
I think if TV did not exist
Life would take a terrible twist
We love films, sport and shows
It's amazing how TV can make your mind grow.
My mum said TV is a daily treat
If my homework is nice and neat.

Joe Stapleton (10)
Larmenier & Sacred Heart RC School

Running Through The Field

Running through the field
The ball comes to my feet.
Here I go, going towards the goal
To shoot and put it in the net.
Then here I am celebrating my goal
When I trip up and say, 'Doh!'
But the other team then start without me
On my half and also fast
But then I am embarrassed
And say I'm such a big old tart.

Chaudien Mwalimu (9)
Larmenier & Sacred Heart RC School

My Little Dog

My little dog
jumps like a frog.
He is very fast
but always last.
His green eyes
are cold like ice.
He wakes me up in the morning
with his snoring.
Then we go for a walk
before seven o'clock.
When I come back from school
we play in the pool.
He loves to swim
with a fin.
He sleeps in my room
with a little broom.
He is my best friend
and our friendship will never end.

Dominic Waluszewski (9)
Larmenier & Sacred Heart RC School

The Dove

High in the clear blue sky,
Flies, with a message of love,
A beautiful white dove.
It soars with majestic delight,
Bringing great tidings of peace
Day and night.

John O'Neill (9)
Larmenier & Sacred Heart RC School

The Seasons

Spring, spring, glorious spring
When the birds sing
Gathering twigs for their nest.
Mother Nature at her best.

Summer, summer, bright and light
Let's all have a water fight.
All outside having fun
While we dance around the sun.

Autumn, autumn, look at the trees
With yellow, brown and crispy leaves.
Watch as they flutter down
Kick them all around the town.

Winter, winter, wear a scarf
Throwing snowballs is a laugh.
Joy and happiness everywhere
Buying presents at the Christmas fair.

Oliver Hart (8)
Larmenier & Sacred Heart RC School

Excitement - Haiku

Excitement is life,
It is having a cute dog!
I'm sure to have one.

Emma Mitchell (8)
Larmenier & Sacred Heart RC School

Me And My Little Pony

Me and my little pony
with his four legs
and a belly as big as powder kegs
enjoy each other's company every day.

But every time I go for a ride
my pony neighs and kicks the air
and down on the grass I slide
oh how unfair, how unfair!

But one of these days
I am gonna tame my pony
and we will enjoy
each other's company even more!

Stefan Camber (8)
Larmenier & Sacred Heart RC School

My Mum

My mum is very nice
I know she likes eating lots of rice
She is very tall
But I know I am very small
She likes seeing a waterfall
And she is very cool
When I sit on a stool
Maybe she is pretty
Because she has lots of pictures.

Lucie Nagy (8)
Larmenier & Sacred Heart RC School

The Many Colours Of Yorkshire

*(I stayed in a cottage in the Yorkshire Dales at half term
and this poem is about all the lovely colours of the countryside there.)*

Sheep as white as snow,
Dogs as black as a storm,
Leaves as green as grass,
Sky as blue as the sea -
The many colours of Yorkshire.

Bricks as brown as a fence,
Buttercups as yellow as bananas,
Sunshine as orange as a lion's mane,
Roses as red as rubies -
The many colours of Yorkshire.

Fraser Gibbs (8)
Larmenier & Sacred Heart RC School

Fear

Fear is black
It tastes like bitter poison
And smells like rotten eggs
Fear looks like a girl trapped in a cave
Fear sounds like a baby screaming
It feels like pure pain
Lots of people feel fear
But luckily you don't!

Amira Campbell-Zeid (8)
Larmenier & Sacred Heart RC School

Lonely Nothingness

The cries of the wind
whistles in your ear

The smell of sand
as it flies up your nostrils

The never-ending hills
in a deserted desert

The soft yellow sand that covers your feet
feels like a broken cushion.

The bitterness of particles
filling your mouth.

Naomi Bharwani (10)
Larmenier & Sacred Heart RC School

My Family

My family are very important to me
They treat me like a baby
My grandad, my cousins, my mummy and my daddy
They all care for me.

I love them dearly
They make me happy and fill my heart with joy
Although sometimes I just moan and annoy
With all my heart I am nothing but a wonderful boy.

Benito Leus III (8)
Larmenier & Sacred Heart RC School

Eight Today

Golden, flickering flames
just waiting to be blown out . . .
one, two, three, four, five, six, seven, eight . . .
Whoosh!
A delicious chocolate sponge cake
with cocoa icing as black as night.
Glittering dust shimmering, like frost in wintertime.
The rich, sweet smell of chocolate cake.
Mouth-watering sweets, all the colours of the rainbow
in every shape possible.
Happy birthday to you Claire -
hip hip hooray!

Maria Howard (8)
Larmenier & Sacred Heart RC School

London Bridge

I stand on London Bridge,
the silent blue river drifts away,
birds are tweeting the lovely songs they sing,
a breeze whistles through the trees,
several boats float by
and the burning red sun twinkles in the corner of my eyes,
the river is dirty and horrid as usual,
but the view is more than you could wish for.

Lauryn Pierro (10)
Larmenier & Sacred Heart RC School

Up On Stage

On the stage I just stare,
as the beady eyes look,
but as I start to sing,
people cheer in gladness,
opening my drip lips
I say a word and a sudden silence
comes from the crowd,
feeling sparkles in my back,
I twitch on the stage,
but as I dance
I sweat like a man jogging around the world,
seeing them looking as if I were a cat,
I tell my joke
and people suddenly laugh out loud!

Donn Guray (8)
Larmenier & Sacred Heart RC School

Bang!

Bang! A blow-out,
Rubber went flying,
My sister was crying.
It surprised us all.

Screech! Brakes on full,
The lorry stopped,
Its tyre had popped,
Surrounded by a cloud of smoke.

Blast! The driver shouts,
He was nearly there,
That's not fair.
Glad it wasn't us!

Thomas Fee (8)
Larmenier & Sacred Heart RC School

Ingredients To Make A Beach

Take one beach,
Pour on some golden sand,
Scatter on some shells,
Scramble on some picnics,
Sprinkle on some people
And mix for five minutes.

Stir in shimmering blue water,
Mix in melting ice cream,
Place in the sound of children laughing,
Carefully place in some sandcastles,
Then drop in some rock pools
And that is how you make a beach.

Molly Gurney (8)
Larmenier & Sacred Heart RC School

Football In The Park

Once in the park I was playing with my mates
On the pitch right next to the big park gates.
The score was equal until I shot,
My team cheered but the keeper did not.
The weather was perfect, all hot and sunny,
When I tripped over they all thought it was funny.
The match finally ended and our team won,
Everyone agreed that we'd had fun.

Michael O'Connell (8)
Larmenier & Sacred Heart RC School

Christmas Time

C hrist our Saviour was born on Christmas Eve,
H aving family to celebrate as they take some leave.
R oast turkey and Christmas pudding is the food of the day,
I wish I could learn to skate on ice, that's what I say,
S o my dream on Christmas Day is for soft snow to fall
T hen my friends and family would enjoy throwing snowballs
M aybe with help I'd learn to skate, oh what fun it would be
A wish like this to come true would be the one for me
S till it might happen next Christmas - let's see

T ime as well for giving and sharing is an important issue;
I know greeting lost friends will bring out many a tissue -
M y Christmas dream would bring happiness to each child,
E veryone loves to get out so long as the weather is mild.

Brigid McMorrow (7)
Larmenier & Sacred Heart RC School

The Forest

The forest is green and bright with the colours of the rainbow.
Rivers shine and flowers blossom.
The grass grows, trying to reach the sky.
The trees grow wildly and the birds sing loudly.
Foxes come out of their caves, hunting for food
Soon it gets dark so the animals sleep with the shine of the moon.

Sofia Rodrigues (8)
Larmenier & Sacred Heart RC School

Snowflakes

S nowflakes cover the streets like a blanket
N ow is the time to have fun with our friends
O n the snowmen we put hats, gloves, a scarf
                      and a carrot for a nose
W inter is the season of snow and Christmas
F lakes fall from the sky slowly to the ground
L ittle children listen our for Santa's sleigh
A very snowy winter has come
K ids run around with happy smiles on their faces
E veryone makes snow angels in the ground
S now is a wonderful time in winter!

Odegua Williams (10)
Larmenier & Sacred Heart RC School

My Disneyland Poem

Disney is great
Disney is fun
Disney is full of laughter
With people having lots of fun.

Disney characters are always around
Laughing, jumping to the music around.

The streets are full of magic
With the parades going up and down
But we have to say goodbye for now
And we will see you very soon.

Amy Hagan (8)
Larmenier & Sacred Heart RC School

Chopin

Chopin is the boy's name,
Piano was his fame.
He lived in a faraway land
But his music echoed across Poland.

He played on the piano,
Full of emotion and stress
And, as a result
I think he is the best.

What else can I say apart from his fame,
That he is always standing
On my mantelpiece
And guiding my way.

And now I can honestly say,
That without his notes,
My life would really
Be in pain.

So hopefully with God's help
And His big grace
I think one day
I may be the same.

Karol Rybarczyk (10)
Larmenier & Sacred Heart RC School

Saturday Morning

Saturday morning, up I get,
Toonatic's on the TV set,
Brush my teeth, wash my face,
Check that everything's in place.

I love this day,
It's the best,
Cos I get to play footy,
So I'd better get dressed.

Francis Edwards (8)
Larmenier & Sacred Heart RC School

Ice Cream

I love to sit and dream,
about delicious, tasty ice cream.
I love it when it's warm and sunny,
to eat the cool ice that fills my tummy.
In a cone or tub,
strawberry or chocolate, it's gorgeous grub.
I love to have it after dinner,
pistachio flavour, now that's a winner.
It is my favourite, I cannot lie,
I'm not keen on cake, custard or pie.
I would love to see a big long stream,
full of chocolate, raspberry and vanilla ice cream.
I have to say it's heavenly to eat,
the beautiful taste you just cannot beat.

Eleanor Hare (7)
Larmenier & Sacred Heart RC School

The Dreamland

In the dreamland
you can swim in the sea.
In the dreamland
you can play with me.
In the dreamland
you can dance all night
instead of lying in bed with a fright.
The dreamland can tell you answers
that you've been looking for,
if you want to be a dancer
just hop onto the dance floor.
If you come with me
you can really see
the magical land of dreams.

Sophie Castillo (9)
Larmenier & Sacred Heart RC School

The Courageous Climber

I'm at the foot of an enormous mountain,
Like a ferocious monster leaning over me,
Overwhelming me,
Nervously I start my ascent.

Halfway now . . . oops . . . I nearly fall,
And suddenly, as everyone looks up,
I find my courage,
I scramble and clamber up.

Tired and alone, my bones feel weak,
I stretch my arms and cling on for survival.
At last I reach the peak,
I jump for joy, I made it!

John Henry Howard (10)
Larmenier & Sacred Heart RC School

Hallowe'en Night

Incy Wincy Spider went out to trick or treat
On Hallowe'en night with eight slippers on his feet
He was dressed up as a circus clown
With a bright red wig and a beautiful gown
Oh what a sight he was to see!
He crawled slowly from house to house
Hoping that no one would shoo him out
Then along came a boy dressed up as a ghost
And stepped on poor Incy like a piece of toast
Oh what a sight he was to see
All squished on the pavement - oh dear me!

Julian Alegre (7)
Larmenier & Sacred Heart RC School

Beware Of Greeks Bearing Gifts

Beware of Greeks bearing gifts,
most people believe it's just a myth.
I believe it is true just as the sky is bright blue,
to know such stories from ancient times,
allows me to make my historical rhymes.
Those ancient heroes such as Achilles,
I'm sure he liked his red-hot chillies.
Odysseus was more cunning and clever,
than most of the rest put together.
Ajax was tall and very tough,
and as he fought he was considered very rough.
Most of all, that was gloriously tall,
stood a great big wooden horse
which would make Troy's walls fall.
Beware of Greeks bearing gifts.

Kristina Novakovic (9)
Larmenier & Sacred Heart RC School

Hallowe'en

H ow scary ghosts are.
A vampire always has fangs.
L ots of sweets on Hallowe'en.
L oads of ghosts wander about on Hallowe'en.
O n Hallowe'en it is very scary.
W itches ride broomsticks at midnight.
E veryone gets sweets on Hallowe'en.
E ven the scaredy-cats go out on Hallowe'en.
N o vampires get scared.

Louise Walsh (7)
Larmenier & Sacred Heart RC School

The Game

The name of the game
scares anyone who plays it.
The game keeps them in a dusty cage.
The game is so scary it can take a life.
Whoever enters the game
will be dead in less than half an hour.
The game is the king of kings in the games.
No game can challenge the mighty game.
It is like twenty lions ready to attack
anyone who dares comes face to face.
Will bow down with no words.
The game comes to life at midnight.
If you buy the game
you are in the hands of the game.
You never know
the game can turn on you
wherever you go!

Oluwafemi Fadeyi (9)
Larmenier & Sacred Heart RC School

Winter

Winter is cold.
Winter has snow.
People make snowmen.
Lots of people get ready to receive treats from Santa.
People buy presents.
But most of all, December is the birthday of Jesus.

Olivia O'Sullivan (8)
Larmenier & Sacred Heart RC School

I Love My Dad

I love my dad,
He isn't bad.
He cares for me,
As you can see.
I'm all alone and frightened,
But when he comes, I lightened.
I call him Daddy,
'Cause he makes me happy.
Yes, I need him,
He has a friend called Tim.
He isn't hairy,
Or scary.
But he loves me,
The way I love him.
Happy birthday to him,
Come on, let's have a drink.
Hip hip hooray,
I do really love my dad.

Louise De Thomasson (9)
Larmenier & Sacred Heart RC School

The Winter Days

The animals are off, off to their bed,
'We're off to hibernate,' the hedgehog had said.

The long summer days were gone,
The days were short and the night came fast.

The very cold days were coming quick,
For the children were wrapped up, in coats so thick.

Agatha Warren (8)
Larmenier & Sacred Heart RC School

The Pitstop

Drive fast, faster,
Blurred faces cheering,
Must drive faster.

Need fuel, need fuel,
Must slow down,
Brake hard,
Stop just there.

Fuel please,
Tyres please,
Quick as you can,
Need to drive fast.

Pitstop over,
Back on the track,
Drive fast, faster.
I win!

Benedict McGonigal (7)
Larmenier & Sacred Heart RC School

Flower

I saw a flower,
A beautiful flower,
Blooming day by day,
Brighter and brighter it got,
I hoped it would stay.
It could have been a gigantic flower,
The biggest in the land.

Ellie Merron (8)
Larmenier & Sacred Heart RC School

Bailey

I love it when she's on my bed,
all warm and sweet,
she behaves so well I give her a treat.
She likes to snuggle her warm soft muzzle
on my feet, what a treat,
she loves to nuzzle.
She is still a puppy, only 7 months old,
though she is good she still needs to be told.
She gives you her paw
and sits and stays well,
we hope she continues,
only time will tell.
She is a bull mastiff,
a rather large breed,
so we need a rather large collar
and a pretty strong lead.
She is part of the family,
we love her so much,
she is cute and cuddly
and soft to the touch.
She loves her walks,
we take her out daily,
this is our puppy dog,
our puppy dog, *Bailey*.

Rebecca Hare (9)
Larmenier & Sacred Heart RC School

October - Haiku

Red, yellow, brown, gold,
Autumn leaves drifting from trees
Crunch under my feet.

Flora Fergusson (9)
Larmenier & Sacred Heart RC School

The Spartan War

Dating back from a long time ago
The Spartan warriors were not slow
I'm here to tell you about a story
Based on a war that was very gory
With King Leonidas, big and strong
His enemies won't live long.

In Xerxes' battle
Sparta lost some cattle
But King Leonidas
Didn't need this
So instead he stood and fought with 300 Spartans
But there were none named Martin.

He killed many soldiers from the Persian empire
But a village from Sparta was set on fire.

On the 4th day of fighting
In Sparta they were writing
That the King was dying
And there was no one left to do the crying
Then a colossal amount of arrows were shot into the sky
And Xerxes said bye-bye.

The arrows blocked out the sun
And King Leonidas tried to run
But he was done for
Still there was a war
Finished by 40,000 Spartans
Still with none named Martin.

Leandros Philiotis (11)
Larmenier & Sacred Heart RC School

Lion

L urking in the grass
I n a flash they are gone, they're so fast.
O n the zebra it goes,
N ow it is time to sleep and rest its toes.

Niall Walsh (11)
Larmenier & Sacred Heart RC School

Scuba Diving

I'm moving gently forward,
over the wild and unexplored world below me.
I'm floating in silence
and breaking it up with the sound of my breath.
Above me there's nothing but shimmery light,
the place where I have come from
and will go back to when I am done here.

I am diving,
I am a scuba diver.
I'm going deeper past the wrinkled rocks and dark seaweed,
toward a deep blueness,
where a shoal of fish await.
As I swim through the water
bubbles burst from me,
wobbling like little jellyfish as they rise.

I check my air,
I don't have as much time left as I need
to see the open breeze in the place where I have come from.
I then give my review to all people I know
who love the wild underworld beneath us.
I hoped I would do it again . . .
and I did!

Natalie Kelly (10)
Larmenier & Sacred Heart RC School

The Farm

Uncle Toby had a farm.
Sleepy pigs slept in the barn.
Grumpy sheep in the field never did as they were told.
The cow that saw the pretty mouse, that tried to go into the house.
Whilst the chicken laid an egg, Auntie Sofie danced the reggae.
The beautiful birds flew in the sky.
All the animals would say goodbye!

Julia Trudu (8)
Larmenier & Sacred Heart RC School

There Is A Dragon On My Roof

There is a dragon on my roof
He's really big and fat
He hates all the birds and bats
There's a dragon on my roof.

There is a giraffe on my roof
She's very, very tall
Yesterday she nearly made the sky fall
There is a giraffe on my roof.

There is a monkey on my roof
He leaves banana skins everywhere
It's like we are at a banana fair
There is a monkey on my roof.

There is an elephant on my roof
He stamps all night
He has got a lot of might
There is an elephant on my roof.

There is a lion on my roof
He is really, really loud
He never ever stops talking
So you always hear a sound
There is a lion on my roof.

There is a dragon, a giraffe, an elephant
A monkey and a lion
In my bed!

Jerina Neli (7)
Larmenier & Sacred Heart RC School

Wonders Of Nature - Flowers

Flowers sprout beautifully all day
The sun shines on them and they brighten up like sparkles
Flowers grow beautifully day by day
They are pretty and smell so nice like perfume.

Theresa Boyo (8)
Larmenier & Sacred Heart RC School

The Cold Autumn Day

As I walk to school on a cold autumn day,
I watch the trees in the wind gently sway.
I see the leaves fall slowly onto the ground,
Whilst I run through them, *thump, pound!*
I start to walk again, I'm out of breath,
And I look up at the trees, where are the leaves?
There are none left!
They are all in the air or under my feet,
So I stamp on them, one by one,
Oh what a wonderful treat!
Orange and brown and other colours so great,
I'll examine them closely, I don't care if I'm late.
They sound so crispy when they crackle and break,
And I laugh quietly and think, *never again will I use a rake.*
I am now at school and in my seat,
And I say to the leaves, under my breath,
'After school again we will meet.'

Grace Galbraith (10)
Larmenier & Sacred Heart RC School

Tearful

Tearful is the colour of white
Tearful tastes like a salty ice cube melting on my tongue
It sounds like a drop of water dripping down from a tap
It looks like a piece of snow falling down from a holly tree
And smells like some sea salt.

Amy Cavanagh (8)
Larmenier & Sacred Heart RC School

The Urban Fox

From the moment that I saw him,
in the early morning mist,
he was just a fox, or so you might say,
to me, he was special at the start of my day.

I looked into his dark fiery eyes
they hooked me like I was hypnotised.
He was an outlaw on our dark and dreary street,
as I walked on to school, wondering who he would meet.

He seemed like he was forgotten from an old mystery story.
He didn't look like he was sad
but neither was he happy.
He was just a mystery in our busy London world.

Calypso Eaton (9)
Larmenier & Sacred Heart RC School

I Have A Dream . . .

I have a dream about a world,
where we all are united,
in peace, love and friendship,
without wars and unnecessary hardship.
I have a dream that . . .
nature will be protected,
peace and love will be promoted,
every child will be educated
and, a better world will be created.

Joseph Ejere (7)
Larmenier & Sacred Heart RC School

The Ferry Ride

When we go to France we go on a ferry,
Up and down, side to side, oops there goes my belly.
We go outside to see how fast we are going,
Wind in my hair, a splash on my belly.
Walking around you can't stand still,
Wibbling, wobbly, just like a jelly.
We get to our feet to have something to eat,
And our dinner ends up at somebody's feet.
We sit on a chair and play solitaire,
The boat gets really rocky and knocks over Daddy's coffee.
We go to the shop to buy some pressies,
By the time I get out I feel like a battered teddy.
We sit down and rest, I don't feel my best,
I hope we get there soon because I feel like a balloon.

Jamie Storer (7)
Larmenier & Sacred Heart RC School

Hallowe'en Poem

When we were little
instead of trick or treat
we would say pick a sweet.
When we saw a pumpkin
we would say it was big, orange and neat.
When we saw a witch
we would say what a sneak
she'll steal our sweets.
When we saw a vampire
we would say beware of his teeth.

Daniel Alegre (7)
Larmenier & Sacred Heart RC School

How I Love My Brand New Class

How I love my brand new class
I am settled and happy at last
My concentration has got so good
I am doing what I should
I have made new friends, but I have old friends too
I have the same teacher, she is not new
I like my new class, I am doing well
At reading, maths and I like to spell
My mum, dad and family have seen me improve
I am very happy that I have been moved.

Maia Ferguson (8)
Larmenier & Sacred Heart RC School

When A Fairy Visited Mum

When my mum had just turned four
She saw a fairy knocking at the door
The fairy shone and really glittered
She waved her wand and shimmered and flittered
The fairy sat and talked with Mum
She stayed all day and had great fun.

Grace McWeeney (7)
Larmenier & Sacred Heart RC School

Hallowe'en

At Hallowe'en monsters are seen,
Gary the ghost, I like the most,
Vlad the Vampire likes to scare,
Sammy the Skeleton has no hair.

Winnie the Witch has a green toad,
I like to watch the fireworks explode,
I go to funfairs with very high rides,
My little sister likes the slides.

Soon Hallowe'en ends,
I go back to school to see my friends.

James Ireland (9)
Larmenier & Sacred Heart RC School

My Cat Lettie

My cat Lettie is a funny cat
she loves water
and sits in a little green basket.

My cat Lettie is a silly cat
she plays with a yellow ball
and gets really excited.

My cat Lettie
I love my cat Lettie
and I always will.

Stella Smith (9)
Larmenier & Sacred Heart RC School

Winter

Snowflakes gently fall to the ground,
The blanket of snow on the ground deepens.
Wind bites and stings your face,
As it rushes into you.

Children in woolly hats and gloves,
Throwing snowballs joyfully around the park.
People on sledges race down steep slopes,
Seeing who can win the race.
Skaters smoothly skate over the ice,
As they move about like professionals over the shimmering ice.
That's winter.

Thomas Whear (10)
Larmenier & Sacred Heart RC School

Rain

When you're walking in the street
and you haven't brought an umbrella,
watch out for rain!
You shouldn't, wouldn't want to get wet.
It isn't nice, it doesn't happen twice.
We've tried to remember; it didn't help.
You should've, would've brought an umbrella.
Now you've soggy socks, and you'd better dry them off!

Isabella Curtis (9)
Larmenier & Sacred Heart RC School

The Cheeky Cat

There once was a cat who lived in a hat
Nibbling an old Christmas pie.
He found a gold crown and then he sat down,
He broke it too and it made him frown.
He stood up straight-backed as he looked back
Wondering what to do.
Out of the corner of his eye, he spotted the pie,
What a good plan he seemed to have found.
He'd stuck the gold crown back together
With the gooey pie that had gone brown.

Natalie Barroso (9)
Larmenier & Sacred Heart RC School

Autumn

The leaves are turning orangey-brown,
Ready to fall onto the ground.
They spin and twirl in the air,
Falling down everywhere.

Conkers crack open when they hit the ground,
Children picking, all around.
Squirrels collect conkers and all
Ready for their winter store.

George Whear (7)
Larmenier & Sacred Heart RC School

Guinea Pigs

G uinea pigs are sweet
U nder and
I n my shed they go
N ibbling and
E ating carrots
A nd cabbage

P ick them up, they wiggle and tickle
I t feels soft and scratchy
G uinea pigs like stroking and cuddles
S ugar is my guinea pig's name!

Isabel Cook (7)
Larmenier & Sacred Heart RC School

The Blue Poem

The sea is blue,
Some birds are blue,
Your eyes are blue,
I have a blue toy,
Blue, blue, blue,
I like blue,
It is in my heart,
My favourite colour is blue.

Melanie Espinosa (8)
Larmenier & Sacred Heart RC School

The Sun

The sun lights up the whole world
The sun is orange because it is hot
The sun is a big ball of fire that is very hot
The sun is getting hotter every day.

Lequain Matthew (8)
Larmenier & Sacred Heart RC School

The Day At The Zoo

I went to the zoo
First I saw a kangaroo
To the tiger I ran
He could eat a man!
Then to the penguins we went
On the fence we leant
And we watched them eat fish from a dish.
It was time to go home
Oh how the time had flown!

Matilda Cook (9)
Larmenier & Sacred Heart RC School

Toys

We all like toys when we buy them,
But how long will they last?

One day you'll get a toy,
And one day you'll give it away!

How much does it cost?
How much is it worth?

Think, do you really want it,
Or will you give it away?

Cameron Steel (10)
Larmenier & Sacred Heart RC School

The World

Clouds go past in God's clear sky.
The birds all around do fly.
The butterflies rest on flowers and trees.
The crabs crawling from the sand to the sea.
People around who care and are kind.
Tomorrow, who knows what we will find.

Francesca Vernazza (7)
Larmenier & Sacred Heart RC School

Football

F ootball!
O n with the kit
O nto the pitch
T actics discussed
B eat them we must
A t the blow of the whistle
L egs fly like missiles
L ong shot at goal

I t bounced off the pole
S econd half beckons

G oal scored in a second
R esult, now we're winning
E ighty thousand fans singing
A nd when the game's done
T he match we have won!

Joseph McWeeney (9)
Larmenier & Sacred Heart RC School

Mountains In Wales

Wind blows as the flock of sheep eat the sweet grass
and the rabbits run in a flash,
as the rock climbers walk steadily to the top
and wind blows as the days go by.

Joseph Ragheb (9)
Larmenier & Sacred Heart RC School

Excitement

Excitement is the colour of the rainbow.
It tastes like the best chocolate cake in the world.
It feels like your best friend is coming to play on the PlayStation
And scoring a winning goal, in the school playground.

Miguel Navarro-Alvarado (9)
Larmenier & Sacred Heart RC School

Happiness

Happiness is the colour bright yellow,
It tastes like a juicy apple,
It looks like my family's smiling faces,
It sounds like some birds singing in a tree.

Georgia Novell (8)
Larmenier & Sacred Heart RC School

There Is A Dog . . .

There is a dog, it looks like spice,
It eats this kibble that is full of rice,
It barks and scampers whenever you open the door
And lives in my house where it licks its paws,
It fills me up with happiness and joy,
When it chews and plays with its cuddle toy.

Stephanie Christenson (7)
Norland Place School

Leopard

Live on land that is dry
Or sometimes in a pond I lie
I am now sleeping on a mound
Eating some food I have found
Food is always on my mind
It's true I am not very kind.

Imogen Ginty
Norland Place School

Glamorous Giraffe

I am a giraffe running gracefully through a glade,
I am one of the beautiful things God has made.
I'm as tall as a tree,
You'll never be as tall as me.
I'm far off the ground
And hardly make a sound.
I have a black tongue
And rather smelly dung!
I am very, very spotty
Or you might call it dotty.

Helena Peacock (7)
Norland Place School

Lovely Leopard

A leopard creeping through the bush in the hot air,
Spotty, soft with silky fur and a scary glare.
Leopard, leopard so hard to see,
I think I see him in a tree.
Sleeping softly, dreaming of tender meat,
I think it's quite a treat.
I'm sorry to say I must go,
Grr, I am afraid so!

Raphaella Redfern
Norland Place School

The Leopard In The Bush

A leopard is scary.
A leopard is pretty with a lot of dots.
Leopards are born in a den, out of the hot.
Leopards run very fast when they hunt for food.
Some of the other animals think they are rude.

Emilia Kalff
Norland Place School

Crocodile Attack

It looks like a log
It lives in a bog
It has a bumpy back
Good when it wants to attack
You don't want it to sit on your lap
Otherwise *snap, snap, snap!*
When it is in the water it's fast
But on land, that's hard to grasp
It lives in the heat
And loves lots of meat!

Georgina Lloyd Yorke (7)
Norland Place School

Are You Scared Of Leopards?

Spotty and furry
Elegant and purry
Doing its run
In the fading sun
It lives in a den
With babies, about ten
Eating juicy meat
Makes him feel neat.

Stella Boden (7)
Norland Place School

Dolphin Life

I live in the ocean down in the sea plants,
And sometimes when I'm mad I do a little dolphin dance.
I need my meal to keep me big,
Sometimes it's hard when the little fishes do a jig.
I make a funny sound when I jump up high,
But sometimes I'm in the ocean looking up in the sky.

Georgia Colfer (7)
Norland Place School

Blue And Green

I saw a zebra blue and green,
Its eyes were black and white,
Its furry skin was so very clean,
I have to say quite bright,
It centred swiftly on its hind feet,
It stopped and looked at me,
Together we sat and took a seat
And there we sipped some tea.

Maddie Dye
Norland Place School

The Swimming Rainbowfish

The rainbowfish swims in the sea,
Colours everywhere shining at me.
When I see them they swim away
It will make me want to stay.
Maybe they will give a wave
And then they swim through the cave.
It eats little foods like plankton so green,
So small and barely seen.

Lola Rawding (7)
Norland Place School

Galloping Zebra

I'm a zebra black and white,
Eating grass, it's nice and light.
Galloping swiftly through the night,
Living in Africa where it's nice and bright.
It's quite relaxing in a way,
Which makes me feel happy and gay.
I munch grass and it makes a sound,
When I hear it I want to pound.

Charlotte Soanes (7)
Norland Place School

Snappy Croc

I'm a snappy croc going mad
Trying to catch a fish
I'm so glad, and so sad
I can't eat out of a dish
When I catch meat it goes snap
And sadly that's the end of that
I go into water with a *splash* and *splish*
It can't share its food, it's so delish!

Orla Choo (7)
Norland Place School

The Very Proud Lion

A very proud lion walking through the leaves
A very proud lion scratching his fleas
Looking fierce and proud
And his roar is quite load
He eats juicy meat
And walks on four feet.

Charlotte Benigni (8)
Norland Place School

The Desert Elephant

The herd of elephants stomped through the desert dust
For a little dip in the river
Then just off to the dazzling tree to have some shade
And then to the sparkling river to wade
Each soaks his dusty grey skin
Blowing his trumpet to make a din.

Eugénie Bakker (7)
Norland Place School

Chimpanzee

Swishing and jumping from tree to tree,
Eating nuts as he roams free.
Throwing leaves all around,
A little fruit he has found.
Teasing people and tickling their knees,
Going through the jungle with such an ease!

Helena Gray (7)
Norland Place School

Excitement

Excitement feels like a butterfly fluttering in your tummy.
Excitement looks like a dancing skeleton.
Excitement smells like an ice cream sundae.
Excitement sounds as funny as a crazy monkey.
It tastes like a sweet orange.

Jonelle Awotwi (8)
Princess Frederica CE VA Primary School

Shy

Shy looks like a big dark corner in the middle of nowhere.
It smells like a fat sock with flies flying around it.
Shy tastes like a dead bird skin.
Shy feels like a big piece of hot lava.

Tyrese Miller (8)
Princess Frederica CE VA Primary School

Happiness

Happiness smells like raspberry ripple ice cream with chocolate
and vanilla sprinkles in a big sundae glass with a fan cone.
Happiness tastes like a BBQ sausage
with a lot of juice coming out.
It feels like it's the first day of the holiday.
It looks like your family are all together on a funfair ride
and all have won a teddy bear.
It sounds like fireworks in the air.

Rachel Sung Thomas (8)
Princess Frederica CE VA Primary School

Loneliness

Loneliness tastes like a bit of burnt toast
when you've just been walking in the rain.
It looks like a grown man crying his little eyes out.
Loneliness feels like someone has stabbed you
right through the heart.
It smells like a farm on a miserable windy day.
Loneliness sounds like hundreds of people screaming.

Alice Such (8)
Princess Frederica CE VA Primary School

Loneliness

Loneliness feels like a pot with no water inside.
It tastes like some bitter potatoes in the frying pan.
Loneliness smells like sunflowers rotting away.
It sounds like thin air leaving you.
Loneliness is like feeling a lion's jaw.
It looks like somebody leaving you alone.

Rheshan Thompson (8)
Princess Frederica CE VA Primary School

Excitement

Excitement is beautiful
Excitement is sweet
It tastes like chocolate which you eat
It smells like perfume
Looks like the full moon
And sounds like a funny cartoon
Excitement feels like a cuddly bunny
Eating delicious honey.

Aysha Lohan (8)
Princess Frederica CE VA Primary School

Loneliness

Loneliness looks like a dark empty cabin.
It feels like firelight going out.
It sounds like something going pop.
Loneliness tastes like nothing.
Loneliness smells like a Christmas dinner
when you're not eating it.
Loneliness is boring.

Callum Burch (9)
Princess Frederica CE VA Primary School

Dreamy

Dreamy is like a drip of honey.
Dreamy feels like squishy clouds.
Dreamy looks as if it's Heaven.
Dreamy smells like melted chocolate.
Dreamy tastes like waffles.
Dreamy sounds like a harp being played.

Marko Pavlovic (8)
Princess Frederica CE VA Primary School

Fear

Fear looks like a ghost ripping your soul out.
It tastes like poison.
It feels like a hairy tarantula climbing up your back
and into your ear.
It smells like an underground sewer.
It sounds like children screaming their lungs out with horror.

Jaymie Benka-Davies (8)
Princess Frederica CE VA Primary School

Upset

Upset is as bad as a rabbit dying in terrible pain.
It looks like a dark scary scorpion stinging your poor body.
Upset sounds like being alone in a playground without me.
It feels like you're breaking your whole body.
Upset smells like burning your best ever chocolate mousse.

Teddy Otch-Imack (8)
Princess Frederica CE VA Primary School

Scared

Scared feels like you are very small.
Scared sounds like people screaming.
Scared tastes like blood coming out of my mouth.
Scared smells like a dead rat.

Juan Carvajal Chalmin (8)
Princess Frederica CE VA Primary School

Happiness

Happiness feels like my warm soft blankets
             after coming home from school.
It smells like my mum's home-made rhubarb crumble.
Happiness tastes like yummy Yorkshire ham.
It looks like children riding down the hill at the park on their bikes.
Happiness sounds like the music on my mum's music player.

Ava Ansari (8)
Princess Frederica CE VA Primary School

Laziness

Laziness feels like a dinosaur's rough skin.
It tastes like cauliflower that has gone off.
Laziness sounds like children that are fat and boring to play with.
Laziness smells like people that haven't had a bath in ages.
Laziness looks like a grey stormy day.

Sabrina Wani
Princess Frederica CE VA Primary School

Scared

Scared feels like a big blob of goo.
It tastes like a nightmare going into your head.
Scared smells like a dead fox.
It sounds like a ghost screaming.
Scared looks as ugly as Cinderella's stepsisters.

Magda Panek (8)
Princess Frederica CE VA Primary School

Anger

Anger tastes like twenty dustbins with spiders
and other disgusting insects crawling about.
It looks like someone's head has been cut to pieces.
Anger smells like a bucket of vomit.
It sounds like people wailing as loud as they can.
Anger feels like snails and slugs.

Daniel Oritsebemigho Olubanjo (9)
Princess Frederica CE VA Primary School

Loneliness

Loneliness feels like a toy that was broken.
Loneliness smells like a breeze of perfume.
Loneliness sounds like a car bashing.
It tastes like hot chocolate.
It feels like gooey sauce.

Ashleigh Mundle (8)
Princess Frederica CE VA Primary School

Happiness

Happiness smells like my mum's best perfume.
Happiness tastes like a bar of sweet chocolate.
Happiness sounds like the little red robins singing.
Happiness looks like the sunset.
Happiness feels like a soft blanket.

Ella Clarke (8)
Princess Frederica CE VA Primary School

Happiness

Happiness feels like the sunny beach
and the calm sea coming up to you
and tickling your toes and warming you up.

Happiness looks like daffodils dancing in the breeze
with the birds singing along with the daffodils.

Happiness tastes like chocolate chips
melting in my mouth.

Happiness smells like the fresh breeze
blowing around you, swirling in the field.

Happiness sounds like children laughing
on the beach, having fun in the sea.

Maisie Nutt (7)
Princess Frederica CE VA Primary School

Happiness

Happiness feels like a luxurious cushion on your sofa.
Happiness looks like blooming buttercups on the horizon.
Happiness smells like a blooming rose
in the garden near the pond.
Happiness looks like enchanted birds singing in the trees.
Happiness tastes like delectable chicken on your plate.
Happiness sounds like magnificent creatures
singing charming songs in the autumn trees.

Karina Ruseva (7)
Princess Frederica CE VA Primary School

Anger

Anger feels like a pot of fire burning up inside me.
Anger tastes like an ice cream cone covered in rotten seaweed.
Anger looks like a herd of animals rushing to attack their prey.
Anger feels like females ready to attack.

Israel Awolaja (7)
Princess Frederica CE VA Primary School

Happiness

Happiness feels like daffodils dancing in the breeze.
Happiness feels like dancing with the flowers.
Happiness smells like a beautiful butterfly flying in the sky.
Happiness smells like flower seeds growing.
Happiness tastes like butter melting on toast.
Happiness tastes like burning bread.
Happiness sounds like birds tweeting in the sky.
Happiness sounds like lions roaring for their food.
Happiness looks like beautiful flowers growing.
Happiness looks like roses smelling lovely.

Tabassum Ahmed (7)
Princess Frederica CE VA Primary School

Jack The Poem

Happiness tastes like chicken freshly baked
so someone can eat it.
Happiness smells like daffodils dancing in the sun.
Happiness feels like a golden pot burning inside me.
Happiness sounds like people making friends together.
Happiness looks like the world is created
before the world was born.

Jack Batchelor (8)
Princess Frederica CE VA Primary School

Anger

I can see boiling lava which is about to explode.
Anger tastes like scalding hot chocolate that's about to burn you.
The sound is like a squealing mouse but 1,000,000,000
                                                      times louder.
Anger feels like your fingers are about to drop off.
Anger smells like an old sweaty person.

Tom Smith (7)
Princess Frederica CE VA Primary School

Love

Love is like a hall of hugs and kisses.
Love is as strong as one thousand men.
Love is the king of happiness.
Love can never be broken.
Love is like the most precious and rare jewel you could ever find.
Love sounds like pretty birds singing on a summer morning.
Love looks like a beautiful butterfly.
Love feels like a fluffy polar bear.
Love is like the best thing you can imagine.
Love is the loveliest thing.
Love cannot be killed.
Love can kill.
Love cannot touch my other love.
Love cannot be rude.
Love is the greatest thing ever created.

Ashura Hirose (7)
Princess Frederica CE VA Primary School

Laughter

Laughter feels like a daffodil dancing on the road.
Laughter smells like fire boiling in the wall.
Laughter tastes like cookies cooking.
Laughter looks like a smart man dancing.
Laughter sounds like somebody blowing a trumpet.

Younes Benyamoune (7)
Princess Frederica CE VA Primary School

Darkness

Darkness is like a pot of red-hot flames burning up inside you.
Darkness feels like a touch of evil blood scratching you
every second of you life.
Darkness smells like a pot of an old witch's potion.
Darkness looks like evil crushing towards you.
Darkness sounds like loud, deadly screeching noises.
Darkness tastes like an old smelly sandwich.

Finn Noble (7)
Princess Frederica CE VA Primary School

Happiness

Happiness is like holding a pot of gold on a rainbow.
Happiness tastes like an apple that has been
smothered in chocolate.
Happiness smells like a freshly made doughnut with sprinkles on it.
Happiness sounds like a bluebird singing in the gentle breeze.
Happiness looks like a far off view of the Grand Canyon.

Asher Miller (8)
Princess Frederica CE VA Primary School

Love

Love is someone hugging you so much that it's comfy!
It smells like a soft rose dancing in the soft, gentle breeze.
It sounds like someone telling you something beautiful.
It looks like someone kissing you.
It feels like someone holding your hand so tightly that you
just want to hug them.

La-Tasha Jackson (7)
Princess Frederica CE VA Primary School

Happiness

Happiness feels like daffodils blowing in the blowing breeze as if a ghost were pushing them.
Happiness smells like marshmallows toasting on the fire.
Happiness sounds like birds tweeting in the trees.
Happiness looks like dark red roses.
Happiness tastes like chocolate toffee sweets.

Lilly Smith (7)
Princess Frederica CE VA Primary School

Happiness

Happiness feels like the sunny beach and the calm sea coming up to me and tickling my toes.
Happiness tastes like marshmallows toasting on the fire.
Happiness smells like daffodils dancing in the breeze.
Happiness sounds like birds singing in the treetops.
Happiness looks like a ball of love.

Mahalia Mensah (8)
Princess Frederica CE VA Primary School

Happiness

Happiness sounds like rustles on the tree.
Happiness looks like love in a tree.
Happiness smells like the perfume Paris.
Happiness tastes like caramel chocolate.
Happiness feels like warm water inside of me.

Aimee-Leigh Clare (7)
Princess Frederica CE VA Primary School

Anger

Anger feels like elephants stampeding in the meadow.
It is like dogs barking at cats in the night.
It tastes like a dog biting you on the leg.
Anger sounds like a boy crying in a tree.
Anger looks like people stamping on the floor.

Rebecca Hollely (7)
Princess Frederica CE VA Primary School

Happiness

Happiness brings back memories
of excitement that filled my heart,
when Mum and Dad got married.
Happiness is as precious as a ruby,
desire it and you will find an unspeakable joy.
Come on everyone, let's be happy.

Franz Elliah Gragasin (8)
Princess Frederica CE VA Primary School

Love

Love sounds like sweet, sweet roses.
Love feels like the hot sun.
Love looks like a blue sea.
Love tastes like ice cream with chocolate sauce.
Love is like being at home with your mum and dad.

Paris Brady Daley (7)
Princess Frederica CE VA Primary School

Sadness

Sadness sounds like children crying.
It smells like the salty sea or a piece of bark on a tree.
Sadness feels like a ball that hits your tummy,
Or when you have run into a prickly bush.

Sadness feels like a teardrop falling into your mouth.
It tastes like a bumblebee has just stung your tongue.
It looks like a big drop of water falling on the ground
                                          and floating away.
Sadness is like a wild fox hunting for his supper.

Freya Alexander (7)
Princess Frederica CE VA Primary School

Love

Love feels like smooth chocolate, steaming on your tongue.
Love looks like the heart beating, nice and slow.
Love smells like sweet mangoes in a flowery basket.
Love sounds like birds singing.
It tastes like cold, cold strawberries.
Love is like your family.

Tuwuana Green (8)
Princess Frederica CE VA Primary School

Happiness

Happiness smells like roses floating through the air.
It tastes like really nice honey melting on your tongue.
Happiness sounds like breezy trees following us.
It feels like people dancing on the moon.
Happiness feels like people laughing softly.

Harry Wichman (7)
Princess Frederica CE VA Primary School

Sadness

Sadness sounds like a tear dropped in a puddle
                              by a newborn baby.
It looks like chopped onions that make your eyes water.
Sadness tastes like bitter cheese that rats have been eating.
It feels like a pitch-black raindrop in a box.
Sadness smells like black dust floating in the sky.

Annie Rose (7)
Princess Frederica CE VA Primary School

Laughter

Laughter sounds like zebras crying on the African savannah.
Laughter travels like a cheetah on the motorway.
Laughter smells like fresh morning air in the mountains.
Laughter tastes like the colours of the rainbow.
Laughter looks like whiskers on kittens and mittens on rainbows.
Laughter is like a million kisses in the world.

Georgie Charlton (7)
Princess Frederica CE VA Primary School

Sadness

Sadness sounds like a flood of tears behind me.
Sadness looks like a puddle of see-through tears on the ground.
It feels like a teardrop on my hand.
Sadness smells like salty tears.
It tastes like the saltiest tear in the world.

Estella Meachin-Taylor (8)
Princess Frederica CE VA Primary School

Loneliness

Loneliness looks like a vicious wolf hunting for its dinner
                              in the high mountains.
It tastes like seawater dripping from huge waves.
Loneliness sounds like a dog howling for its life because
                              it has a broken leg.
It feels like a really sharp knife jabbing into you.
Loneliness smells like wounded soldiers.

Jakob Leaf (7)
Princess Frederica CE VA Primary School

Loneliness

Loneliness sounds like silence in a dark, locked room.
It looks like a pitch-black, empty graveyard on a damp day.
Loneliness tastes like nothing.
It feels like you have been taken away from your home.
Loneliness smells like dust and moss.
It is like a bear hunting alone.

Jim Laney (7)
Princess Frederica CE VA Primary School

Loneliness

Loneliness sounds like unhappy children crying.
Loneliness tastes like melting chocolate
                 on a poisoned birthday cake.
It looks like tears on a tree.
Loneliness smells like warm cherries.
It feels like the tears in my eyes.

Ryan Hughes (7)
Princess Frederica CE VA Primary School

Anger

Anger sounds like birds screaming,
wolves howling, windows crashing.
Anger feels like hard walls crashing on my hand
or like my broken hand, like blood dropping on me.
Anger smells like people keep farting,
or rotten eggs dropping on the floor.
Anger tastes like eating a live fish
and the fish is trying to suck your tongue.

Maisie Macarthur (7)
Princess Frederica CE VA Primary School

Love

Love looks like a gold star.
It sounds like singing birds.
Love feels like soft, smooth fur
And tastes like strawberry juice.
Love smells like juicy cranberries.
Love is like caramel circles.

Jerell Jeremiah (7)
Princess Frederica CE VA Primary School

Love

Love feels like home.
It looks like strawberry ice cream.
It smells like sugar or honey.
Love sounds like an owl hooting
And tastes like sweet cherries.

Emma Coles (7)
Princess Frederica CE VA Primary School

Love

Love smells like pink roses picked from the garden.
It sounds like a little lamb that has found its mum.
Love tastes like a cake from people in my family
who are getting married in a little cottage.
It looks like flowers that have just come out.
Love feels like a heart in my hands.

Maya DeCosta (7)
Princess Frederica CE VA Primary School

Anger

Anger sounds as loud as a fierce lion roaring
when it fails to catch its prey.
Anger tastes like stale, burnt toast without any butter.
It smells like a fire that has been burning for 100 years.
Anger looks like loads of monsters rising from the dead.
It reminds me of all the bad dreams I've had throughout my life.
Anger feels as lonely as you being shut in a dark, dark room.
Try not ever to be angry.

Jade Read (8)
Princess Frederica CE VA Primary School

Loneliness

Loneliness looks like a grizzly bear eating a deer.
Loneliness feels like living on the street.
Loneliness smells like a baby's nappy.
Loneliness is like a rotten fish that has not been eaten for two days.
Loneliness tastes like burnt crispy chips.
Loneliness is like a big lonely bear trying to attack you.

Milhaan Wani (7)
Princess Frederica CE VA Primary School

Darkness

Darkness is as black as a scorpion.
It sounds as quiet as a warehouse.
Darkness tastes like a barn, tossed.
It smells like a house that has just been burnt.
Darkness looks like a witch's cloak.
It helps me remind myself when my mum left me all alone.
Darkness feels like some ghosts are going to get *you!*

Bruno Bonacin (8)
Princess Frederica CE VA Primary School

Sadness

Sadness sounds like a frozen mouse in the snow.
Sadness feels like cold ice on your chest.
Sadness smells like nothing.
Sadness looks like the black sky and a teardrop.

Eden McNaught-Compass (8)
Princess Frederica CE VA Primary School

Happiness

Happiness smells like brown toffee melting in a bowl,
Its vast blue swallows you up like a big black hole,
Happiness looks like a ball of your favourite things,
It sounds like birds singing in a tree,
It feels like a teddy in a big woolly jumper,
Happiness tastes like a big sweet that has too much taste,
It reminds me of my friends and family being friendly,
But lastly it makes me feel like a billion sapphires.

Louis James (9)
Princess Frederica CE VA Primary School

Love

Love is as radiant as a red apple,
which is enjoyed by children.
It sounds like someone quietly in bed.
Love feels like Cupid shooting someone
with an arrow in your heart.
It tastes like a marshmallow
melting in your mouth.

Love smells like perfume
spraying in the air.
Love looks like snow
falling down a mountain.
It reminds me of my mum
getting me a teddy when I was four.
Always love your family and friends,
love yourself.

Deanna Webb (9)
Princess Frederica CE VA Primary School

Darkness

Darkness tastes like mud.
Darkness sounds like someone screaming.
It smells like horrible, smelly smoke.
It looks like dark red.
It reminds me of my mum's mum dying.
It feels like someone spying on you.

Shania Alana Andall (8)
Princess Frederica CE VA Primary School

Fear

Fear is a colour darker than jet-black.
Fear is like the loudest scream.
Fear feels like a sharp point.
A sharp point just about to poke me.
Fear tastes like a tasteless rock.
Fear is like a pile of dung.
Fear is like a monster.
Fear reminds me of my brother.

Luke Galvin (8)
Princess Frederica CE VA Primary School

Anger

Sounds like hard beating in your heart.
Anger tastes like raw eggs with cold custard.
Anger smells like the fragrance of sour mustard.
Anger looks like raging fire across the Earth.
Anger reminds me of my worst movie with vampires.
Anger, the colour of anger is blood-red with pitch-black.

Kieran Parchment (8)
Princess Frederica CE VA Primary School

Love

Love is the colour bright rosy-red.
It sounds like a lovely robin tweeting.
The fragrance is like a beautiful rose.
Love feels like the start to a new life.
It looks like a hug from your mum.
It tastes like hot, oozy chocolate mousse.
Love reminds me of a brand new couple.

Sadia Hameed (8)
Princess Frederica CE VA Primary School

Darkness

Darkness is a black voice saying, 'I'.
Darkness sounds spooky
Darkness is damp
It will kill you
It tastes like bitter
It is spooky like London's Dungeon
It smells like anger
It feels like darkness
It is as scary as a night in the cemetery
The sound of darkness is like a whirling tornado coming your way
Darkness reminds me of an old person that's died
And as scary as something dark floating round the room
It feels like pain, like your mum slapping you
You are a danger to people.

Thaion Noel (8)
Princess Frederica CE VA Primary School

Happiness

Happiness smells like a bright yellow sunflower opening up.
Happiness sounds like someone who's won a free trip to Africa.
Happiness feels like a silky, furry, warm, soft blanket.
Happiness tastes like a hard crispy cookie.
It looks like a baby laughing like a crazy monkey.

Vivienne, Caroline & Miranda (8)
Princess Frederica CE VA Primary School

Happiness

Happiness is as bright as bright yellow,
It is as smooth as a cake,
It smells like chocolate,
It feels like joy and the sun,
Happiness reminds me of when I got my dog.

Stanley Spark (8)
Princess Frederica CE VA Primary School

Love

Love is as red as the brightest rose just opening.
It sounds like the ocean breeze flowing.
Love tastes like toffee apples melting in the pan.
It smells like the fragrance of my mum's perfume.
Love looks like a fairground with big rides and swings.
Love brings back memories of sweet dreams
And fun things I've done.
You have love in your heart, believe it.

Marnie Hinds-Jones (8)
Princess Frederica CE VA Primary School

Anger

Anger looks like blood inside you,
It sounds like an over-boiled kettle,
Anger tastes like sprouts but worse,
The fragrance of anger is a pile of dung,
It looks like a very untidy bedroom,
Anger reminds me of losing a football match.

Noah Laignel (8)
Princess Frederica CE VA Primary School

Love

Love is as red as a rose.
Love tastes like a chocolate melting in your mouth.
Love feels as soft as a pillow gliding on your face.
Love sounds like the wedding vows that you say.
Love looks like two children playing.
Love smells like the fragrance of a rose.
Love reminds me of when me and my family went to the park.
Love is a nice feeling.

Valexus Robinson (8)
Princess Frederica CE VA Primary School

Great Danes

Great Danes are so pretty,
Great Danes are so sweet.
But when you leave the table,
There's no telling what they'll eat.

Great Danes do the tango,
Great Danes do it well.
But after two hours,
Their feet start to smell.

Great Danes wash their hair,
Great Danes use shampoo.
But when you say they don't need a bath,
They say, 'I do, I do, I do!'

Great Danes wear make-up,
Great Danes hide it in a pit.
But when they can't find their make-up,
They have an endless fit.

Great Danes are the perfect pets,
Great Danes love to play
And if you really wanted to
You could play with them all day.

Lily Goddard (9)
St Christina's School, St John's Wood

Tick-Tock

Tick-tock goes the clock,
It's time for bed, it's eight o'clock.
Tick-tock goes the clock,
It's not fair that I should stop.
I'm having fun, learning to rock,
I hate the clock!
Tick-tock, tick-tock!

Francesca Histon (9)
St Christina's School, St John's Wood

The Journey

Off we go down the road,
Goodbye house and take care little mouse.
We stop and I start to stare, I see,
Strange things, and to think I was right there.
Off we go again down the road,
I see an old man walking past.
I ask Dad to go a bit fast,
Then I get to an open field
With green, green grass.
Gold and green leaves fall from the trees,
Swirling, twirling around our car.
I see a house in the corner,
I turn and look as we zoom past.
Then we get into a narrow street,
Cats running up to greet.
I clearly don't like this journey.

Serena Eyi (9)
St Christina's School, St John's Wood

School Friends

School friends are there for you
to make sure you stay cool.
It doesn't matter what you do
even if you're in the pool.

School friends are there for you
to make sure you're on track.
It doesn't matter where you are
they'll keep you on your track.

School friends are there for you
to keep your friendship going.
No matter what you say or do
you'll keep your friendship growing.

Molly Costello (9)
St Christina's School, St John's Wood

My Doll

I have a doll I play with,
I comb her yellow hair,
I feel very lonely
When she's not there.

She has her own toy house,
It's made of real wood,
I give her a toy sweet or two,
If she's very good!

If you see her room,
Her wardrobe's nice and neat,
In it you'll see clothes,
That look very sweet.

I hear my mother calling me,
It seems we just said hi!
But now it is time for bed,
I must say bye-bye!

Sashini Ranasinghe (10)
St Christina's School, St John's Wood

Rain

Pitter-patter, pitter-patter,
I can hear the rain.
It's falling on the land
And falling on the grain.

It's not quiet like snow,
But it's not loud like a truck.

Lots of sun if I had wishes,
But it's not so good for the fishes.

Erika Shirai (9)
St Christina's School, St John's Wood

Puppy

My puppy is great,
My puppy has a mate.

You are so fluffy,
Thank God you are my puppy.

You lick me all the time,
I'm happy you're mine.

When I take you for a walk,
I always talk.

Puppy, you are so soft,
I would hate it if you were lost.

Oh puppy, you and me,
Make a great family.

Yasmin Zouheiri (10)
St Christina's School, St John's Wood

If I Were . . .

If I were a painter in a funny mood
I would . . .
Paint a dandelion with faces,
Colour my vases' bases
And sketch with my shoelaces.

But if I were a painter in a sad mood
I would . . .
Paint my garden with snow in May,
Colour all my furniture grey
And sketch my sad face as I lay.

Ines de Larrinaga (8)
St Christina's School, St John's Wood

Baxter Where Are You?

I woke up in the morning, the cage was cold and bare,
Oh! where on earth was Baxter? He simply wasn't there.
I looked in my room, I looked upon the stair,
I really couldn't find him, Baxter wasn't there.

Quick, where is Dad? He must be in the shower,
He said he would come in a quarter of an hour.
Mum said Baxter was lost forever,
But Dad came down and said, 'We must be clever.'

'Where do hamsters like to go?' he said.
'Maybe in the dark or underneath the bed.'
Dad knelt down, dripping wet
And saw the two green eyes of our long-lost pet.

Yoghurt drops were Baxter's delight
And he leapt right out to take a bite,
Dad grabbed him after what seemed like an age
And shoved him back into his empty cage.

Tamsin Taylor (9)
St Christina's School, St John's Wood

London

L ondon is a city, a great big city,
O n so many streets there are flower shops that look so pretty!
N elson's Column stands so tall in Trafalgar Square,
D owning Street houses the Prime Minister
   but not the Lord Mayor.
O h London, I love your marathon race,
   (on your marks, get set, go!)
N ever would I leave you to go to another place!

Ria Piccone (9)
St Christina's School, St John's Wood

A Day With A Mythical Creature

As I was opening the mail,
I thought I saw a sparkling scale.
I opened it up to see what was inside
And I spotted a dragon trying to hide.
It looked at me strangely,
So I started to scream.
It flapped its great wings
And up it flew like a dream.

It went swirling and zooming
Never making a sound,
Flew up to the chimneys, then down to the ground.

So if you ever come across a dragon
You have one thing to hear,
Though they may seem quite fierce,
You have nothing to fear.

Caroline Turner (10)
St Christina's School, St John's Wood

Children Of The World

Children are brown, children are white,
Children are dark, children are light,
Children are tall, children are small.

Children are similar in different ways,
Children are different in similar ways,
Children love and care for their friends,
Children like to walk hand in hand.

And every night
When we turn off the light,
We dream of a colourful place
Where we all live in peace.

Camilla Tacconis (9)
St Christina's School, St John's Wood

If I Were . . .

If I were the snow on a happy day,
I would . . .
Faintly touch your shoulders,
Bounce on your window,
Make you feel warm inside your body.

But if I were the snow on an angry day,
I would . . .
Fall angrily down the sky,
Trap you inside,
Freeze you into ice.

Niku Hessabi (8)
St Christina's School, St John's Wood

If I Were . . .

If I were a dinosaur on a happy day
I would . . .
Give you rides on my back,
Let you play with my young,
Take you rampaging through the forest on a sunny day.

But if I were a dinosaur on a bad day
I would . . .
Squash you with my great big feet,
Munch you and crunch you with my sharp teeth,
Send you flying with a whip of my tail.

Noor Jahanshahi (9)
St Christina's School, St John's Wood

If I Were . . .

If I were invisible and feeling kind,
I would . . .
Leave secret presents and sweets of all kinds,
Love to help you in school exams
With whispers of answers or guiding your hand.

But if I were invisible and feeling mean,
I would . . .
Sneak upon you with a pinch or two,
Listen to your great chats,
Play ghostly music to scare you at night
And give you a fright.

Christina Marris (8)
St Christina's School, St John's Wood

Fireworks

Fireworks, the twinkling night.
Fireworks, an incredible sight.
Fireworks, bombs away!
Fireworks on this dark day.
Fireworks fizz and pop.
Fireworks light then drop.
Fire, the red and yellow glow.
It is the scariest thing I know.

Angelica Maxwell (8)
St Christina's School, St John's Wood

Jaguar's Newborn

Walking on the forest floor,
under a deep dark cave,
there sits a girl jaguar.

She's holding her tummy,
what could be wrong,
is it her time to become a mummy?

When is she coming out,
she's been in there for days,
I have already lost count.

When I visit a few days later
much to my surprise,
there is a litter of spotty pups
right before my eyes.

Ellie Marks (10)
St Christina's School, St John's Wood

Colours

C an you see the turquoise waters?
O ver the sea lays the azure sheet of the sky.
L ayers of different greens in the forest.
O ver the emerald-green canopy.
U nder the rays of the sun.
R adiant colours bloom in all directions.
S ailing silver birds swoop in the sky above.

Katharine Marris (10)
St Christina's School, St John's Wood

Volcanoes

Volcanoes spit crumbs of a cookie.
Volcanoes' mouths explode with juice.
Volcanoes shake off the heat.

Volcanoes crackle their hard teeth.
Volcanoes lick the ground.

Volcanoes blaze across the country.
Volcanoes pour liquid into a cup of earth.

Volcanoes turn the bright lights out.
Volcanoes kick the sun goodbye.
Volcanoes rest and say goodbye.

Sophia Jane Paravalos (8)
St Christina's School, St John's Wood

If I Were . . .

If I were the snow in a good mood,
I would . . .
Dance around you with my cold, icy touch,
Glitter you with my snow ice drops,
Sway, performing a secret dance.

But if I were the snow in a bad mood,
I would . . .
Charge at you with my balls of evil,
Fall off your roof and knock you down,
Bite you with my clear white fangs.

Francesca Morelli (8)
St Christina's School, St John's Wood

Rainbows

R ed like a bird killed by a tragic hunter
red like a volcano about to erupt
red like the cheeks of a child who has played all day
red, the colour of love and passion.

A mber like the sun shining above us
amber like the glint that leaves our eyes
amber like a crackling fire
amber, the colour of light.

I ndigo like a moonless night when everyone's asleep
indigo like my bedroom walls
indigo like a crystal ball
indigo, the colour of wonder.

N avy blue like shimmering water in a clear sea
navy blue like the night sky
navy blue like the deepest ocean
navy blue, the colour of depth.

B lack like the gowns worn at a funeral
black like a cup of morning coffee
black like a girl's silky hair
black, the colour of darkness.

O range like one of the most delicious fruits in the world
orange like a sunset in the deep blue sea
orange like the traffic lights when they are changing
orange, the colour of Hallowe'en.

W hite like the blank page in a novel
white like a blanket of snow rested upon the ground
white like the clouds floating above
white, the colour of purity.

S pring-green like a field of grass
spring-green like a leaf fallen from a tree
spring-green like a blossom which hasn't yet flowered
spring-green, the colour of envy.

Laura Bouhélier (10)
St Christina's School, St John's Wood

Down In The Depths

A fork-tailed creature whizzes past me
A wave of fear engulfs me
I cannot hold my breath much longer
My lungs are screaming from a searing pain

The depths below are dark and murky
I see a shimmering light above
I must summon all of my strength
To reach that light, that life

A school of fish swims over me
I stretch my arms upwards and kick
Bubbles escape my ballooning mouth
But I hold tight to my last breath

One more kick and I break the surface
Gasp for air in short, sharp gulps
The boat's still there, I struggle on
And wash up on the deck like flotsam and jetsam.

Ava Meir (10)
St Christina's School, St John's Wood

Haunted House

The wind howling while the moon is shining
on the roof of the haunted house.
The door creaking as she walks in silently
when *bang!* the door slams behind her.
The archaic floorboards creak, as she explores the house.
Walking up the antique stairs,
voices become louder and louder until she finds a room.
Inside the room, on top of the bed,
lays a paralysed body nodding its head.
The door locked, the body nodding, what should I do?
Frozen with fear, I want to run, help me, my feet are stuck.
I need to escape, to get away from this living nightmare
because I need to welcome the day!

Amanee Ekbal (10)
St Christina's School, St John's Wood

Lost

Isolated . . . surrounded by tormenting fears,
Everything rejects me . . .

When I'm around, the sun spins instead of the Earth.

Green spires tower above me,
The boisterous undergrowth clasps my ankle,
Pulling me down onto the ground below.

As I stumble on deeper into the darkness,
Stop . . .
I cannot go any further, I am tangled up;
Skeleton branches are attacking me . . .

My thundering cries echo in the bare woods
That yearn for total silence . . .

No one responds to my deafening cries.

Definitely lost, I think in a parallel world.
Deep down in the forest.

She might be lost and never be found again . . .

Martha Libri (10)
St Christina's School, St John's Wood

Gracefully
(Inspired by 'Slowly' by Pie Corbett)

Gracefully the swimmer dives down,
Gracefully autumn leaves fall to the ground,
Gracefully snowflakes fall from the air,
Gracefully the wind blows through my hair.

Gracefully the ballerina dances on her toes,
Gracefully the cat licks my nose,
Graceful is the Queen - but the most graceful thing I know,
A swan that is as white as snow.

Nadia Muccio (9)
St Christina's School, St John's Wood

Stalking Tiger

Stalking tiger in the dawn,
Catching food,
For a cub just born.

Stalking tiger in the morning,
Pouncing on prey,
Without a warning.

Stalking tiger in the noon,
Nursing a cub,
With no idea of what will happen soon.

Stalking tiger in the evening,
Being watched,
It will soon be leaving.

Stalking tiger in the dusk,
Lying dead,
In a poacher's van with an elephant's tusk.

Kate Gardiner (10)
St Christina's School, St John's Wood

Dreams

I once dreamed a dream which will never come true,
About something that's been my desire,
Girls come around but eventually say adieu,
I wish a true friendship would transpire.

They say, 'How are you today?'
While they're laughing away,
I say, 'Fine, do you want to play a game?'
They say, 'No way!'
So once again there's no one but me;
Who is to blame?

They treat me like no one and shove me to the ground,
Until one day this girl appeared and became a great friend,
Then I awoke to a sound,
Stating, 'Your friendship's at an end!'

Victoria Harvey (10)
St Christina's School, St John's Wood

The Foxes On The Street

On the misty street,
here comes a fox,
now few foxes follow by,
one by one on the misty street.

Oh no! watch out!
here comes a car,
now few cars follow by,
one by one on the misty street.

Now on the misty street,
it is cloudy,
foxes and the cars,
drivers try not to kill the foxes,
foxes try to run away.

At the sunrise there is a noise,
down the street,
one by one the foxes go,
one by one the cars go,
on the busy misty street
on the Monday morning.

Minami Hashimoto (10)
St Christina's School, St John's Wood

Quickly

(Inspired by 'Slowly' by Pie Corbett)

Quickly is the squirrel running past.
Quickly is the bird flying fast.
Quickly is the ant that crawled on the floor.
Quickly is the hamster scratching at the door.

Quickly is the dancer twirling around.
Quickly is the frog jumping up and down.
But the quickest of all is the dog,
Whose tail swooped past my eye.

Maria Rodriguez (8)
St Christina's School, St John's Wood

All Hope Was Lost

A mother sobbed, her child screamed -
the world was filled with shattered dreams.
A face smothered with blotches,
dotted with delicate tears,
an echoing wail floods my ears.
Their only chance was at great cost,
 all hope was lost.
A tiring journey, sweat trickling down her spine,
she couldn't go any further, she toes a line,
a wilting plant, a skeletal tree,
why can't this world be free?
A never-ending winter - only icy frost,
 all hope was lost.
A broken heart, a burning note,
leading up to a strangled throat;
an unwanted betrayal, a sharpened knife,
the tools that stole a precious life.
I see myself reflected in the river
in which he was tossed,
 all hope was lost.

Callista McLaughlin (10)
St Christina's School, St John's Wood

Raindrops

Raindrops swim down the drains, surf through the misty day.
Raindrops fall upon the panes, wash everywhere.
Raindrops spit onto lanes, empty heavy clouds.
Raindrops parachute over gardens, quench the thirst of grass.
Raindrops tickle the rooftops, splash their chimneys.
Raindrops hit and wet.

Eleanor Shanahan (8)
St Christina's School, St John's Wood

Christmas

Snowflakes are falling,
'Merry Christmas' echoing in the streets,
Bells are tolling
As everyone shivers in their boots.

Stars are twinkling,
Everyone's eating apple pies,
Slurping up every crumb on their plate
And then go straight to bed
To wait for Father Christmas to arrive.

Children straining their eyes to stay open,
But fail five minutes later,
Sweet dreams everyone,
Can't wait till tomorrow.

Wake up at 6am,
Run to the fireplace,
Shiny parcels glittering in the firelight,
Hooray, hooray, Father Christmas found his way!

Amy Pezzin (10)
St Christina's School, St John's Wood

Quietly

(Inspired by 'Slowly' by Pie Corbett)

Quietly the leopard runs.
Quietly the baker makes his buns.
Quietly the buns fill my tum.
Quietly they do their sums.

Quietly the river flows.
Quietly the children tie their bows.
Quietly is Joe falling over his big toe -
But most quiet of all,
The flowers grow along the green brick wall.

Alice Johnson (8)
St Christina's School, St John's Wood

Swiftly
(Inspired by 'Slowly' by Pie Corbett)

Swiftly the swallows cascade down,
Swiftly the robins race through the town,
Swiftly the foxes forage for food,
Swiftly the owl hooted and twooed,
Swiftly, swiftly.

Swiftly the town awakens with pride,
Swiftly the mice scurry and hide,
Swiftly the farmers bound out of bed,
Swiftly the children race on ahead,
Swiftly, swiftly.

Swiftly the mothers brew up the tea,
Swiftly the sand is covered in sea,
Swift is the gull - but swiftest of all,
The greedy gannets as they dive and fall.

Willa Bailey (8)
St Christina's School, St John's Wood

Poetically
(Inspired by 'Slowly' by Pie Corbett)

Poetically trees seem to whisper hello
as the sun shines its beaming smile on the forest.
Poetically a girl waters plants - she's a florist,
the water is giving its first thirst-quenching drops.
Poetically fireworks communicate in bangs, sizzles and pops.
Poetically rush-hour traffic stops,
it's peaceful and quiet as day turns to night.

Poetically comes morning and my first sight
is sunbeams swimming in.
Poetically everything sparkles, even the bin.
Poetic I am, so happy and gay,
But most of all is the memory of each yesterday.

Constance Marzell-Kyme (8)
St Christina's School, St John's Wood

Dolphins

Crashing waves,
A leaping dive,
Fierce rocks ahead,
Will she survive?

Skilful moves,
Lightning speed,
In any race,
She'd take the lead.

A fearful whine,
An answering call,
She's but a baby,
So small, so small.

A group of them,
All huddled close,
That baby needs
But one swift dose

Of their love and care,
Her family, her pack,
Huddled and hidden,
Through a great crack.

She just fits,
Thanks to her size.
Thank goodness that crack
Could compromise.

She's joined the rest,
How happy she is!
How lucky, for the ocean,
She'd be his.

Laura Pujos (10)
St Christina's School, St John's Wood

Surreptitiously
(Inspired by 'Slowly' by Pie Corbett)

Surreptitiously the radiant sun crept behind a bush.
Surreptitiously the kitten clawed its way up a tree.
Surreptitiously the mouse sniffed the salty ocean.
Surreptitiously the robber mourned for gold and jewels.

Surreptitiously the darkness faded to a brilliant blue.
Surreptitiously the lion stole away to devour his delicious meal.
Surreptitiously was the boy muttering to himself
                                      in the desolate streets.
But most surreptitious of all, was the girl copying
                                      her friend's Spanish test!

Lara Meir (8)
St Christina's School, St John's Wood

Quietly
(Inspired by 'Slowly' by Pie Corbett)

Quietly the calm wind blows through the oak tree.
Quietly the yellow leaves fall down on the green.
Quietly many acorns play hide-and-seek.
Quietly a fluffy squirrel collects, gnaws in the cheek.

Quietly a curious boy follows in secret.
Quietly a man on the bench reads a mystery, smoking a cigarette.
Quiet is the woman sleeping beside the man -
But quietest of all,
Autumn comes to my garden without call!

Ryoko Matsuda (8)
St Christina's School, St John's Wood

If I Were A Shape

If I were a shape
I'd be a star.
I'd be a shiny star in the night sky.
I'd be a football player on a football pitch.
I'd be a special star that God sent for shepherds to follow
If I were a star.

If I were an arch
I'd be a mirror in the Queen's palace.
I'd be a bridge in San Francisco.
I'd be a window in my flat
If I were an arch.

If I were a cuboid
I'd be a soft sponge in my bathroom.
I'd be a cage with an ugly parrot inside.
I'd be a wardrobe in a shop
If I were a cuboid.

If I were a circle
I'd be a ticking giant cuckoo clock.
I'd be a hole in a big oak tree.
I'd be a number zero
If I were a circle.

If I were an oval
I'd be a hen's boiled egg.
I'd be a green big balloon
If I were an oval.

But if I were a cone
I'd be an ice cream cone.

Eloi Lopez Rodriguez (8)
St George's (Hanover Square) School

If I Were A Shape

If I were a shape
I'd be a circle
I'd be a little ball bouncing for a goal
I'd be a steam mill trying to race the wind
I'd be a small clock waking people up
If I were a circle.

If I were a cone
I'd be a delicious chocolate ice cream
I'd be a party hat
I'd be a spud's nose
If I were a cone.

If I were a square
I'd be a SpongeBob Squarepants
I'd be a London map
I'd be a birthday present
If I were a square.

If I were a star
I'd be Patrick the starfish
I'd be a twinkle, twinkle little star
I'd be a school batch
If I were a star.

If I were a triangle
I'd be a coat hanger
I'd be a Cheddar cheese
If I were a triangle.

But if I were a cylinder
I'd be a rollie.

Lethaniel Stacey-Coombe (7)
St George's (Hanover Square) School

If I Were A Shape

If I were a shape
I'd be a cone
I'd be a rocket with a sharp red nose
Which shoots off and comes back.
I'd be the end of a tank's gun which shoots missiles.
I'd be a big spike with guns all over it
If I were a cone.

If I were a cuboid
I'd be a huge building, bigger than any school.
I'd be a chimney that had writing on it.
I'd be a robot's head which was bright red
If I were a cuboid.

If I were a square
I'd be a whiteboard with a teacher teaching children about shapes.
I'd be a computer for good children.
I'd be an orange seat for children to do their work
If I were a square.

If I were a sphere
I'd be a globe with a wooden top.
I'd be a big keyhole with a key
If I were a sphere
But If I were a rectangle
I'd be a work bench.

Callum Macleod (7)
St George's (Hanover Square) School

Listen

L istening means your ears are awake.
I f Mr Jones is speaking we should sit up straight.
'S ilence!' he roars at the noisy boys.
'T errific behaviour, Form 3 girls.'
'E leven times six? What's the answer?'
'N ouns, verbs and adjectives
   must be learnt before Monday, please.
   Are you listening?'

Emmeline Crosby (7)
St George's (Hanover Square) School

Cats

A cat sits on a mat.
She sleeps like mad
And if you wake her up
She pounces, not knowing who you are.
Now, she sleeps on her mat very peacefully.

Shrawani Kulkarni (7)
St George's (Hanover Square) School

Listen

L isten, listen, you have to listen
I t is what the teacher said,
'S it and do your work quietly
T alk to no one and don't behave badly.
E nd of the day is when you play
N ow don't be the worst class today.'

Milos Petrovic (7)
St George's (Hanover Square) School

Friends

Friends are as funny as a boy tickling me,
Friends are as caring as me, you'll see.

Friends are as charming as a fish,
Friends are like shooting stars' hearts beating.

Friends are as energetic as Jason Gardiner,
Friends are as friendly as someone raising money for charity.

Friends are happy as the Three Wise Men meeting Jesus.

Friends are as cheeky as a monkey,
Friends are as kind as me, he he!

Christopher Docker (9)
SS Mary & Pancras CE Primary School, Camden

Friends

Friends are as helpful as a computer,
Friends are as pretty as a rose,
Friends are like glowing sparkly stars in the sky,
Friends are like black cats,
Friends are like a cheeky monkey that is chunky,
Friends are as tall as a giraffe,
Friends are as fun as a roller coaster.

Maisha Akter (8)
SS Mary & Pancras CE Primary School, Camden

My Friends

Friends are like a life of joy.
Friends are as fabulous as the sun.
Friends are sparkling diamonds.
Friends are as fantastic as the moon with wonderful sparkles.
Friends are always as sunny as a sunflower
And as special as the Queen.

Rebecca Ahmed (9)
SS Mary & Pancras CE Primary School, Camden

Friends

Friends are like happiness in each and every way,
Friends can make you happy even on a sad day.

Friends are like family, they always help you out,
They will be there when you need them and they will
                                            never ever shout.

Friends are like a nurse, they never let you down,
You can always trust them, they will never let you frown.

Friends are smart, they help you on a test,
Friends are always there, they are better than the rest.

Libby Habib (8)
SS Mary & Pancras CE Primary School, Camden

Friends

My friends are as helpful as a computer.
My friends are as shiny as a wrapper.
My friends are like Heaven with a sweet angel.
My friends are like fireworks glittering down the sky.
My friends are as sweet as an ice cream cake.
My friends are as shiny as a coffee
And some sprinkles of gold and some sugar.
My friends are like happiness.

Hicham Medjebour (8)
SS Mary & Pancras CE Primary School, Camden

Friends

Friends are like chocolate,
Chocolate is like my mum.
Chocolate is my life,
Chocolate is my favourite.

Friends are like chips,
Chips are like yummy things.
Chips are like Miss Feller,
Chips are my dream.

Friends are like my mum,
My mum is like my cousin.
My mum is like my baby nephew,
My mum is like a famous person.

Friends are teachers,
Teachers are like helpers.
Teachers are my favourite people,
Teachers are the best.

Friends are like helpers,
Helpers are helpful.
Helpers are kind,
Helpers are wonderful.

Friends are like a butterfly,
Butterflies are beautiful.
Butterflies are lovely,
Butterflies are kind.

Friends are like Jesus,
Jesus is helpful.
Jesus is handsome,
Jesus is as lovely as a bird.

Friends are like Santa,
Santa is kind.
Santa is wonderful,
Santa buys presents.

Friends are like my family,
My family is happy.
My family is great,
My family is clever.

Shannon Phelan (9)
SS Mary & Pancras CE Primary School, Camden

Friends

Friends are like family.
Family is like a big band.
Family is like a big school.
Family is like swimming.

Friends are like chips.
Chips are like making.
Chips are like making fun things.
Chips are the being beautiful.

Friends are like my best teacher.
My best teacher is like my mum or dad.
My best teacher's a professional singer.
My best teacher is like playing out.

Friends are like chocolate cake.
Chocolate cake is like chips.
Chocolate cake is like a drink.
Chocolate cake is like lots of food.

Friends are like a drink.
A drink is like school.
A drink is like my brother.
A drink is like making a chair.

Friends are like going to the park.
Going to the park is like seeing someone I know.
Going to the park is like having fun.
Going to the park is like getting an ice cream.

Ellie Thompson (8)
SS Mary & Pancras CE Primary School, Camden

Friends

Friends are like sunflowers, they never stop giving,
They keep on doing it, it's like they work for a living.

My friends are as sweet as a sweet, *mmm!*

My friends are like stars, they never stop their shine,
I'm so happy that they're all mine.

My friends are warm and fuzzy, fuzzy as a bee,
The funny thing is they do it for me.

My friends are as tall as a flower,
They are so tall they're just like a tower.

When my friends are sorry,
They're as cute as a puppy.

My friend's eyesight is as good as an eagle,
But I guess it's because they eat lots of bagels.

Venetia Williams (8)
SS Mary & Pancras CE Primary School, Camden

Friends

Friends are like sparkly stars in the sky
and they wave bye-bye.

Friends are like chocolate cake,
they are baked with chocolate milkshake.

Friends are like chocolate muffin,
they are baked in a Hallowe'en cookie.

Friends are as smart as a bat
so let's pick up a smart cat.

Samiya Rahman (8)
SS Mary & Pancras CE Primary School, Camden

Friends

Friends are like smiley faces like me.
Friends are as strong as John Cena.
Friends are like birds flying in the sky.
Friends are as smart as a computer.
Friends are like chocolate ready to be eaten.
Friends are as cool as me.
Friends are like scientists about to do experiments.
Friends are like fireworks banging in the sky.

George Yoxall (8)
SS Mary & Pancras CE Primary School, Camden

Friends

Friends are like a star in the classroom,
Friends are as kind as a teacher,
Friends are as helpful as a teacher's assistant,
Friends are as smart as a giant's computer brain,
Friends are as cheeky as a cheeky monkey,
Friends are as beautiful as Beyoncé,
Friends are a champion,
Friends are my best friends!

Salma Siddika (8)
SS Mary & Pancras CE Primary School, Camden

Friends

Friends are as kind as a teacher, they can never stop.
Friends are like chocolate ice cream, I feel like eating them.
Friends are as strong as John Cena because
                              they are good at football.
Friends are as beautiful as a puppy.
Friends are as smart as a teacher.
Friends are as pretty as Miss Feller.

Abby Webster (8)
SS Mary & Pancras CE Primary School, Camden

My Best Friend

Chattering and chuckling,
All through the day,
She is kind and nice,
In every single way.

Lovely, nice,
Kind and caring,
Telling secrets,
Always sharing.

She's the best,
We're friends forever,
All the time,
We stick together.

Tara Steeds (9)
Tetherdown Primary School

Racing Cars

R ushing fast,
A fter first place,
C heers filling the air after them,
I n a car going so fast,
N ot going to crash they hope,
G lad they're doing so well,

C heers even louder now,
A nd they're all nearly there now,
R ipping drivers' nerves,
S ome drivers lifting trophies.

Zak Tait (9)
Tetherdown Primary School

Rabbit Kennings

Fun jumper.
Nice player.
Lawnmower.
Pellet eater.

No sleeper.
Night runner.
Day rester.
Burrow maker.

Veggie ruler.
Ball player.
Tunnel runner.
Tube tunneller.

Bunnies.

Matthew Wickham (9)
Tetherdown Primary School

Friendship Poem

Forever friends
Our friendship never ends
Stay together
Always with each other.

Sweets we share
Don't tell anyone else
Always happy
Happy playing around.

Saskia Epstein-Tasgal (9)
Tetherdown Primary School

Anger

What colour is it?
It's red like blood.

What does it look like?
It looks like a tiger taking his prey.

What does it sound like?
It sounds like a volcano crackling to burst.

What does it taste like?
It tastes like burning coal.

What does it smell like?
It smells like being trapped in a room of smoke.

What does it feel like?
It feels like touching some burning hot metal.

What does it remind you of?
It reminds me of all the bad things I have ever done.

How does it make you feel?
It makes me feel very sad and unwanted, so lonely.

Madeline Buttling-Smith (9)
Tetherdown Primary School

Happiness

Happiness looks like the sun, a yellow bowl of fun.
Happiness sounds like the laughter of children playing.
Happiness is bright yellow.
Happiness tastes like a delicious chocolate pudding.
Happiness reminds me of the best times of my life
                        when I went on holiday with Harry.
Happiness makes me feel all tingly inside.

Sebastian Jowett (9)
Tetherdown Primary School

The Tornado

The sky is grey and the clouds are thick,
There's loads of hail and the wind's blowing quick . . .
I snatch the remote and start to click.

The dark sky roars like a lion in a fight,
There's a loud crackle and out goes the light . . .
I check what's on the TV tonight.

Now the wind forms into a cone,
In a few seconds the cone has grown . . .
I switch off the TV and walk to the phone.

Now the cone has started to bend,
Spinning like it will never end . . .
I dial up a number and call up a friend.

A fence collapses and some tiles blow off a roof,
A car is lifted up and past flies a boot . . .
I sit on the sofa and wobble my tooth.

I walk to the window and look out,
Surprised and shocked, I give a shout,
'Watch out everyone, there's a tornado about!'

Robert Johnson (9)
Tetherdown Primary School

Darkness

Darkness is black like a clear night sky.
Darkness sounds like a grey wolf howling.
Darkness tastes as bitter as beer.
Darkness looks like a pitch-black room with no exit.
Darkness feels like there's no one else in the world.
Darkness.

Ben Long (9)
Tetherdown Primary School

Adding Another To My Collection

They're all boxed,
Laid in rows,
What's inside
No one knows,
Each of them has some connection,
Adding another to my collection.

Now it comes to choosing one,
Or two, or three, or four,
Or maybe five, or six, or seven,
Or eight, or nine, or more,
Different figures of different sizes,
Until one catches my eye and rises,
In my hand towards the counter,
Stored in each a little section,
Adding another to my collection.

Ben Hodgson (9)
Tetherdown Primary School

Dying Flower

Crying and crying, moaning and moaning,
Hopelessly dying from time to time,
Looking around, groaning and groaning,
Petals crunching, losing their shine,
The flowers swaying from side to side,
Curling away, trying to hide.

Silently weeping and weeping,
Carefully, slowly dropping their seeds,
Sadly sleeping and sleeping,
Folding up their lovely leaves,
Petals falling to the ground,
Creating a ginormous mound.

Julia Zlotnick (9)
Tetherdown Primary School

The Tornado Is Coming

I went to the window
and gazed at the sky
There was greenish weather
the thunderstorm is nigh
Then suddenly lightning struck
The drums of thunder rolled at night.
A burst of hail and a violent change of wind
The tornado is near, I started to shout.

The swirling, the whirling and that curling.
The tornado was fast and furious.
There was a loud roar
and then a scream.
The tornado started gathering speed
It ruined all the houses and darted all the seeds.
The sky was dark
The tornado gave a loud screech
then started dying down
Like the calling of a hound.

Defne Navaro (9)
Tetherdown Primary School

Sadness

Sadness feels like the ice-cold sea.
Sadness looks like fuzzy blue dots.
Sadness tastes like sour lemon juice.
Sadness makes you feel like you're isolated in a box.
Sadness smells like smoke being blown in your face.

Murray Boyle (9)
Tetherdown Primary School

A Pony For Life

I wish I had a pony with a really long black mane.
It would be extremely fun.
I'd put him in a shelter when there was rain.
I'd let him in the field when there was sun.
I'd play with him in a meadow
And groom him twice a day.
What fun it would be to have a pony for life
With a really long black mane!

Greta Shrimpton-Phoenix (9)
Tetherdown Primary School

Love

Love is red like when the bright sunset goes down.
Love smells like a beautiful red rose.
Love reminds me of my family and friends.
Love looks like a beautiful red heart.
It tastes like delicious strawberry jam.
It sounds like lovely, happy, playful children having fun.

Cameron Wells (9)
Tetherdown Primary School

Darkness

Darkness,
Darkness is the colour of the pitch-black sky
And sounds like the roar of a killing lion.
It tastes of sadness and anger.
It smells of saltwater, from a polluted river.
The sight of it is gloomy and dark.
It feels like frustration and punishment.
It reminds me of a hideous monster
And makes me feel, empty.

Alice Martin (9)
Tetherdown Primary School

Sausages

S izzling, soft, squidgy stuff,
A ll rolling about in the pan,
U nder one another all the time,
S uch tasty meaty puffs.
A ll are pink, I must eat them,
G rab them tasty things,
E at them up right now,
S orry, you can't have one, they are all gone *now!*

Benjamin Levine (9)
Tetherdown Primary School

Trance Limerick

There was a young man from France
Who acted as if in a trance
Until someone went click
And his brain went tick
And he decided to do a small dance.

Elinor Gibb (9)
Tetherdown Primary School

Steak

S ucculent sizzle
T ossing and turning
E xciting meat
A mazing taste
K etchup, anyone got any?

Leo Style (9)
Tetherdown Primary School

Mountain

```
       M M
      O   O
      U   U
      N   N
      T   T
      A   A
      I   I
      N   N
```
I go climbing
Over rocky gravel
S   l   i   d   i   n   g
Climbing   up   and   up
I've got hot tea in   my cup
My   blisters   all   go *pop, pop, pop*
Yeah! Look at me, I've gone and reached the top!

Joseph Humphreys (9)
Tetherdown Primary School

Land Rover

L uxurious
A ll terrain
N eat interior
D rive of a dream

R ugged
O ff road
V ehicle
E verlasting
R ide of a lifetime.

James Hall (9)
Tetherdown Primary School

Joy

What colour is it?
Joy is yellow like a very hot fire.

What does it look like?
It looks like a hot, sunny day.

What does it sound like?
It sounds like a happy dog barking.

What does it smell like?
It smells like burnt toast on a Saturday morning.

What does it feel like?
It feels like soft silk sheets.

What does it remind me of?
It reminds me of a bouncy castle.

Milo Nesbitt (9)
Tetherdown Primary School

Jermain Defoe

J uggling jumper
E xciting shooter
R idiculously good goals
M agnificent striker
A mazing interceptor
I ncredible goal scorer
N ice penalty taker

D efoe star
E cstatic boots
F ootball player
O h, good goal
E xtremely good shots.

Jules Marks (9)
Tetherdown Primary School

The Seaside

Swift swimmers swimming,
Perfectly positioned pier,
Shiny, sizzling sun,
Curly, climbing clouds,
See-through silly starfish,
Playful people playing,
Scary sharp-toothed sharks,
Flying, fighting fish,
Soft, smooth sand,
Perfect, protruding pebbles,
Salty, shallow sea,
Big, beautiful boats,
Fine floating floats,
Red rubber rings,
Clean, colourful costumes.

Laura Latter (8)
West Acton Primary School

Young Writers Information

We hope you have enjoyed reading this book - and that you will continue to enjoy it in the coming years.

If you like reading and writing poetry drop us a line, or give us a call, and we'll send you a free information pack.

Alternatively if you would like to order further copies of this book or any of our other titles, then please give us a call or log onto our website at www.youngwriters.co.uk

**Young Writers Information
Remus House
Coltsfoot Drive
Peterborough
PE2 9JX
(01733) 890066**